i

Researching UX: Analytics

by Luke Hay

Copyright © 2017 SitePoint Pty. Lt

Product Manager: Simon Mackie   **Technical Edit**

Series Editor: Joe Leech   **Cover Designer.**

English Editor: Ralph Mason   **Author Photo:** Will Barnes

Published by SitePoint Pty. Ltd.

48 Cambridge Street Collingwood
VIC Australia 3066
Web: www.sitepoint.com
Email: business@sitepoint.com

ISBN 978-0-9943470-7-7 (print)

ISBN 978-0-9953827-0-1 (ebook)
Printed and bound in the United States of America

About Luke Hay

Luke Hay is a UK-based UX Consultant who's been working with websites since the 1990s. He prides himself on taking a user-centric, analytical approach to design, development and optimization of websites and apps.

Luke currently splits his time between working as the Senior Conversion Strategist at integrated digital agency Fresh Egg, and as a freelance UX and analytics consultant and trainer. Always involved in his local digital community, Luke has helped organize and curate events for UX Brighton, and is one of the organizers of UX Camp Brighton. You can find out more about Luke at www.lukehay.co.uk.

About SitePoint

SitePoint specializes in publishing fun, practical, and easy-to-understand content for web professionals. Visit http://www.sitepoint.com/ to access our blogs, books, newsletters, articles, and community forums. You'll find a stack of information on JavaScript, PHP, Ruby, mobile development, design, and more.

This book is dedicated to the Brighton UX community. Thanks for your support.

Table of Contents

Chapter 3   An Introduction to Analyzing Data 49

Chapter 4   Finding Problems with Analytics 70

Chapter 6   Measuring and Reporting

Outcomes...128

Preface

Good UX is based on evidence. Qualitative evidence, such as user testing and field research, can only get you so far. To get the full picture of how users are engaging with your website or app, you'll need to use quantitative evidence in the form of analytics.

This book will show you, step by step, how you can use website and app analytics data to inform design choices and definitively improve user experience. Offering practical guidelines, with plenty of detailed examples, this book covers:

- why you need to gather analytics data for your UX projects
- getting set up with analytics tools
- analyzing data
- how to find problems in your analytics
- using analytics to aid user research, measure and report on outcomes

By the end of this book, you'll have a strong understanding of the important role analytics plays in the UX process. It will inspire you to take an "analytics first" approach to your UX projects.

Who Should Read This Book

This book is for UX professionals, designers, product managers, and anyone interested in using an analytics tool to improve UX. No prior experience with Google Analytics or other analytics tools is assumed.

Conventions Used

You'll notice that we've used certain typographic and layout styles throughout this book to signify different types of information. Look out for the following items.

Tips, Notes, and Warnings

Hey, You!

Tips provide helpful little pointers.

Ahem, Excuse Me ...

Notes are useful asides that are related—but not critical—to the topic at hand. Think of them as extra tidbits of information.

Make Sure You Always ...

... pay attention to these important points.

Watch Out!

Warnings highlight any gotchas that are likely to trip you up along the way.

Supplementary Materials

- https://www.sitepoint.com/community/ are SitePoint's forums, for help on any tricky web problems.
- **books@sitepoint.com** is our email address, should you need to contact us to report a problem, or for any other reason.

Chapter 1

Why Analytics?

> Without data, you're just another person with an opinion.
> — *W Edwards Demming*

Analytics is an often overlooked area of UX. This book will help you understand how an analytics-first approach to UX will enable you get great results. I'm not suggesting that you use analytics to replace your other UX methods, but instead that you combine analytics with other UX methods to create an excellent user experience.

In the first chapter of this book, we'll look at why analytics data is important when it comes to evaluating user experience. We'll then move on to how to check that your analytics data is accurate, and how to go about analyzing it. The second half of the book focuses on how to use analytics to find problems, how to use your data to aid your user research, and how to use analytics tools to evaluate and report on the success of your design changes.

By the end of this book, you'll have a good idea of how to use your website analytics to make informed decisions about the design of your website or app.

The Importance of Analytics for UX

Good UX is based on evidence. This is often qualitative (qual) evidence, such as observations from usability testing or findings of field research. Using only qualitative evidence, though, means overlooking a huge amount of quantitative (quant) data that may be available to you. Quantitative data is primarily numerical and can be measured. This is often used in the form of website analytics, and can be even more compelling than qualitative evidence. Later on in this chapter, we'll look in more detail at how the two forms of analysis are defined and what they entail.

It's not a case of using one form of research and analysis: qual and quant go hand in hand to give a rounded picture of the overall user experience.

The diagram below shows how analytics can inform other user research methods:

1-1. Where analytics fits in with some common user research methods (credit: Tim Minor)

As the diagram shows, the landscape is made up of both qualitative and quantitative methods. Both make up crucial parts of user experience research and design. They give different forms of insight that are crucial for getting a rounded picture of the user experience of a website or app.

Put simply, the quant side of things will generally tell you *what* users are doing on a website; the qual side of things will help you to find out *why* those things are happening.

Advantages of Using Analytics in Your UX Process

Web analytics should be a vital part of your UX process. However, you may not be aware of all the reasons why you should include a quantitative approach to your work. In this section, I'll cover five advantages of using analytics information to shape your UX recommendations.

1. **Analytics provides facts that are hard to argue with.**

The data that comes from website analytics software is not subjective in the same way that qualitative data often is. While forms of qualitative research are open to interruption, the metrics used in website analytics are more black and white. This leads to fewer arguments about the findings.

As this quant data is definitive, it also makes it perfect for measuring the impact of changes. If a design solution to a problem is implemented, it can be measured by analyzing the changes in user behavior before and after the change was made. This makes it easier to prove your point and show the value of your work.

2. **Analytics gives fast results.**

Analytics can often give an almost instant answer to a question. Other forms of user research can take days or weeks to produce results, but accessing quantitative data can be as easy as opening your analytics package and navigating to the right report. As mentioned previously, I'm not advocating using only a quantitative approach, but if time is short, it may not even be possible to use other UX methods. You can get a good overview of user behavior on a website within minutes using the right analytics tools and techniques.

3. **Analytics offers unique insight.**

There is a huge amount of information available from your web analytics package. In Google Analytics alone there are around 80 different standard reports made up from over 400 different dimensions and metrics, and that's before you event start to create your own reports. No other UX methods can give you as much data.

Also, as website analytics are constantly collected, you have a full overview of how a website is being used over time. Other methods tend only to show a snapshot of how users are engaging with a site over a particular period. Analyzing data that has been consistently collected over time gives much more insight than one-off studies.

4. **Analytics combines well with other UX methods.**

As you'll find out later on in this book, analysis of your analytics data can fit in at various points during your UX process. Data sourced from your analytics can pinpoint problem areas on your website that can then become a focus for usability testing, heuristic assessments, or any other form of qualitative research.

Demographic information can also be taken from analytics to help build up your personas and to provide the basis for user research or usability testing recruitment. If you're evaluating user journeys, website analytics can play a central role in showing you how people are currently navigating your website. Finally, as touched on before, analytics data can be used to measure the impact of any design changes you make. Analytics data can enhance almost every aspect of your UX work!

5. **Analytics offers an effective way to present your findings.**

Presenting findings of UX work to stakeholders can be difficult. Getting across the results from long-term field studies, for example—in a way that stakeholders can relate to—can be a challenge. Analytics data naturally fits into presentations. This relates to point 1—that analytics data is hard to argue with. The "black and white" nature of analytics means that you have "hard" data to show stakeholders and clients. This can be particularly useful for demonstrating the difference that your UX efforts have made, and even showing the ROI of your work. Also, clients and stakeholders love a graph!

Arguments Against Using Analytics

Hopefully I've convinced you that analytics should play a key role in your UX work. Just in case you still have any doubts, though, here are some of the common arguments against using analytics, along with an explanation of why they're all wrong.

1. **Analytics devalues other UX work.**

Some people are concerned that using quantitative data dehumanizes users and takes away from the purpose of UX. This would be true if quantitative data were used on its own. But as long as it's used to support qualitative methods, there's no negative impact of using analytics data. Quantitative analysis will tell you *what*, but not *why*. That's why it can't be used in isolation. It serves to *inform* other UX work rather than to replace it.

2. **Quantitative analysis takes a certain mindset.**

   I've heard people claim that they don't have the right type of mind for analytics, and that they're "not good with numbers". I don't believe that's the case at all. I wouldn't consider myself to be naturally analytical; I never did well with mathematics at school, and it's not an area I've always wanted to work with. Analyzing metrics relating to how people use a website isn't rocket science. The analytics software does most of the number crunching for you. Nobody's going to ask you to come up with complicated formulas or have an in-depth knowledge of statistics, and you don't have to be a full-time data analyst to get great insight from your data. The real skill is in knowing where to look and how to interpret reports. If you can navigate a website and pull out the key information from it, you can do web analytics.

   Once you understand the basics, you'll be surprised how easy analyzing your website analytics actually is. The people I meet in the UX industry tend to have a broad skill set across a range of different disciplines, so adding analytics knowledge to that shouldn't be too challenging.

3. **Learning analytics is too difficult.**

   Following on from the previous point, developing a good understanding of web analytics really isn't that difficult. Learning some basic principles will get you a long way. If you already have a good idea of the data you want to find, then a basic understanding of how to use a web analytics package will be all you need to get started. There is also lots of support for analytics packages available online. Google Analytics has the excellent Google Analytics Academy[1], a free resource containing hours of instructional videos. Then, of course, there's this book, which will show you how use your analytics knowledge to aid your UX process.

4. **It takes too long to set up.**

[1.] https://analyticsacademy.withgoogle.com/

Some people believe that it takes too long to set up web analytics, integrate it and gather enough data. Even if you're starting completely from scratch, you should be able to set up analytics software on your website very quickly. It's often as simple as spending five minutes setting up an account, and then a couple more minutes adding a line of code to your website. You can set up analytics on a website in the morning and have access to visitor data by the afternoon. A more advanced, bespoke setup may take a bit longer—but no longer than many other forms of analysis. Setting up a usability testing session, for example, can take days. Also, once your analytics software is set up correctly, it will constantly deliver useful data with very little maintenance.

5. **It only shows data on website/app visitors.**

The fact that website analytics only contains data from people who visit your website or app is a limitation. You won't be able to find any data in your reports about potential users, and, as a result, you'll only get part of the picture. This brings us back to the first point, though. This book is not about convincing you that you should only use quantitative data. Instead, it's about how you can use quantitative data to inform your qualitative work.

Defining Qualitative and Quantitative Data

Hopefully the previous pages have convinced you that analytics will help you improve your UX process, and you're now keen to get started. Before you dive into your analytics, let's have a look at what we mean when we talk about quantitative and qualitative data. The table below gives an overview of the two terms.

	Quantitative	Qualitative
Concerned with	Discovering facts	Understanding behavior
Data analysis	Numerical comparison	Themes identified by users
Insight	How much of a behavior is present in a group	What factors determine the behavior in a group
Reporting	Statistical inferences	Language of the users
Example	Web Analytics	User testing

1-2. The difference between quantitative and qualitative data

Quantitative data is anything that can be "quantified". This type of data is normally presented in the form of numbers, and is used for discovering facts. Examples of quantitative data are things like the number of visits to your website, the amount of time people spend on your website, and the amount of purchases users make on your ecommerce website.

Qualitative data cannot be expressed as a number. In UX terms, qualitative data often centers around understanding behaviors or attitudes based on observations. This could be from user research, and is more open to interpretation than quantitative analysis. Other forms of qualitative analysis include stakeholder interviews, immersive research and heuristic assessments. Qualitative data is generally used to find out *why* something is happening.

Both types of data are valid types of measurement, and both should be used during the UX process. The real skill is knowing which type or method to use to achieve your particular UX goal. Remember, though, that quant and qual compliment each other, so rather than using one or the other, use both.

Quantitative Methods

Quantitative UX methods are used to get an understanding of *what* is happening with a website. They seldom tell you much about the motivations and motives of your users, but they can be used to get a good understanding of what they are doing on your website. Some typical examples of quantitative methods include:

- web analytics
- form analytics
- heatmaps
- A/B testing
- eye tracking
- click testing
- surveys (can be quant and qual)

These methods will help to get a great understanding of what people are doing on your website. The data provided by these quantitative methods will help to build an understanding of where you might want to focus your efforts on improving your website.

Both quant and qual are vital for a rounded UX approach. This book will focus on how you can use your quant data to inform your qual work. It's all about taking an "analytics first" approach to UX.

Qualitative Methods

Qualitative UX methods take many forms, and are often used for building an in-depth picture of your users. They are typically used to help you find out *why* something is happening. Some typical examples of qualitative methods include:

- usability testing
- ethnographic/field studies
- focus groups
- diary studies
- screen/session recording
- user feedback
- stakeholder interviews

- immersive research
- design workshops
- heuristic assessments

These methods will help to get a great understanding of your website users. The level of detail provided by these qualitative methods will help to build empathy with your users, and will give a good understanding of why they behave the way they do. This book is not about these types of methods, but it will reference them to show how they can be informed by quantitative data.

A Look at Some of the Analytics Tools Available

The final section of this chapter covers some of the different analytics tools that are available. This is not intended as an in-depth review of each option, but instead gives an overview of the pros and cons of each. Remember, the tool you use is less important that how you use it.

A lot of analytics tools provide similar reports to each other. Website analytics tools, for example, will normally show you the similar data in a similar format. The majority of the techniques covered in this book can be achieved using a combination of the tools that are covered below.

Website Analytics Tools

The most commonly used type of quantitative tools are website analytics tools. These tools will tell you, amongst other things, how many visits your website has received and what pages those users viewed.

Google Analytics

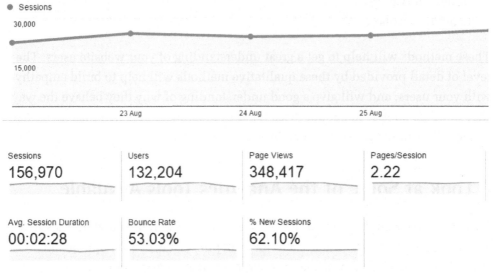

1-3. A screenshot showing the overview report in Google Analytics

With around 50 million users, Google Analytics[2] is the most widely used website analytics service in the world. The service was launched in 2005 after Google acquired website statistics analysis company Urchin. In 2012, Google launched Universal Analytics, which uses a more flexible tracking code and enables cross-device tracking. The tool is set up on a website by adding a snippet of JavaScript code to every page.

Pros

There are several advantages to using Google Analytics as your analytics tool. One of the most compelling reasons to use Google Analytics is the fact that it's free. There is a premium, paid-for version available, but this is only recommended for websites that receive millions of visitors a month. You're paying for the tool to handle more data and for dedicated technical support. The free version will be the best option for the majority of us, and it provides almost all the functionality of the premium version, so you're not really missing out on anything by using the free version.

---

2. https://analytics.google.com/

Google Analytics is very easy to set up, too. Anyone can register for an account, and the setup process just involves adding a simple snippet of code to every page of your website. While customization of your account is recommended, just adding the code to your site will mean that you have access to the majority of the standard Google Analytics reports. You can get the basics set up and begin tracking visitors within about ten minutes of creating an account.

Though no customization is required to use Google Analytics, it's recommended for getting the most out of your data. There are many customization options that will help you improve your reporting and ensure it's relevant for your requirements. Google Analytics is easy to customize, allowing users to set up their own goals, dashboards and custom reports. You can even import data from other sources and analyze it alongside Google Analytics data.

As touched on previously, Google Analytics is the most widely used analytics service in the world. This means that it's very well supported. Google itself provides excellent tutorials and documentation, and many independent analysts, including me, regularly blog about how to get the most from Google Analytics. If you want to focus on one website analytics tool, Google Analytics is a good choice, as you're likely to encounter it on many other sites. It's like choosing to learn a language that's spoken in lots of countries.

As the tool is constantly being updated, it means useful new features are launched regularly. One example of this is the recent introduction of the User Explorer reports, which allow you to analyze the behavior of individual (anonymous) users over time. This is a very exciting development for us UXers.

Cons

There are few disadvantages of using Google Analytics. One of the main disadvantages is actually a side effect of one of the advantages. The fact that Google Analytics is updated regularly means that useful new features become available. However, updates to the Google Analytics interface and reports mean that you need to use it regularly to stay on top of these changes. If you don't access your Google Analytics account regularly, you may find yourself lost when you log in after some time away and find yourself presented with unfamiliar-looking reports.

The accuracy of Google Analytics data has been called into question. This is a particular issue for smaller websites, where inaccurate numbers may not be representative of trends. Reasons for a lack of entirely accurate data include users with JavaScript or cookies disabled not being counted, and cookies timing out due to user inactivity. Despite this, Google Analytics is still considered to be one of the most accurate reporting tools. However, you'll need to keep in mind that no analytics tool is ever going to be 100% accurate 100% of the time.

At the other end of the scale, larger websites may run into data sampling issues. Data sampling is an analysis technique that analyzes a smaller set of your data in order to identify larger patterns and trends. Google Analytics uses data sampling to speed up the performance when dealing with a large amount of data. This can lead to accuracy issues and inconsistent results.

Another issue for some is that you need to allow Google access to your data. While this is not a problem for the majority of website owners, there will be cases when this is not desirable.

The use of ad-blocking software has also led to users blocking their data from appearing in Google Analytics. Some ad-blocking tools will block Google Analytics by default, while many others can be set up to block Google Analytics tracking at the click of a button. This problem is not unique to Google Analytics, but it's an issue that you should keep in mind when analyzing your data.

Finally, Google Analytics relies on users having JavaScript and cookies enabled. Only around 1% of users have JavaScript disabled, so this isn't a big issue, but it should still be taken into consideration. It's a similar issue for users who disable cookies. This may be a small number, but if it's important that you track as many visitors as possible, you might want to look into alternative tools such as Piwik.

Adobe Analytics

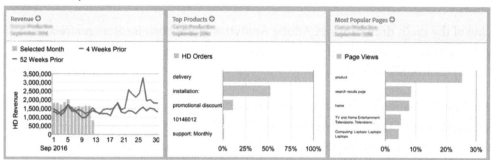

1-4. A screenshot showing Adobe Analytics

Adobe Analytics[3] (previously Site Catalyst) is a set of tools for predictive and real-time analytics. It has a lot of similarities to Google Analytics in terms of its reporting functionality. It's less commonly used than Google Analytics; around 360K sites use it globally, though it's used by a lot of high-traffic, high-profile websites.

Pros

Adobe Analytics is sometimes seen as the better choice for websites with a lot of traffic. Google Analytics will sample data if there's a large amount of traffic. Sampling data can lead to inaccurate reports, which can potentially be a big issue.

The tool is almost infinitely customizable. This means that, when it's set up correctly, it can give you almost all the data you'll ever need. To create the optimum setup in Adobe Analytics, three components have to be configured: business objective implementation, technical implementation, and end-user understanding/training. If you can crack all three, then Adobe Analytics can be an immensely powerful analytics tool.

Adobe Analytics also integrates out of the box with other Adobe marketing tools, making it an attractive choice for companies who are already using Adobe products.

[3.] http://www.adobe.com/marketing-cloud/web-analytics.html

Cons

One of the main drawbacks of Adobe Analytics is the cost. It offers no free version, unlike Google Analytics, and the cost of accessing the tool is likely to be tens of thousands of dollars.

Another big issue for Adobe Analytics is that there's no out-of-the-box interpretation of the data. Reports—particularly the custom insight variables—differ from implementation to implementation. This means even if you master the setup of one Adobe Analytics account, you may be completely stumped by another. Adobe Analytics is a powerful tool, and with this comes the need for training and external support.

Adobe Analytics requires a fair bit of configuration. This means that setting up the tool for the first time can be a lengthy and complicated process.

Other Notable Web Analytics Tools

There are several other analytics tools available. These include Piwik[4], Clicky[5], Kissmetrics[6], Woopra[7] and Yandex Metrica[8].

Some tools work similarly to Google Analytics and Adobe Analytics, while others collect data in different ways. Piwik, for example, is an open-source analytics package. It enables website owners to install the software on their servers and use it to interrogate web log data. This means that it can be run without JavaScript tracking, unlike other major analytics tools.

Yandex Metrica is an interesting tool. It's currently free to set up. As well as giving standard website analytics, it also offers heatmapping and session recording, where users' visits are recorded and can be watched back on video.

[4.] https://piwik.org/
[5.] https://clicky.com/
[6.] https://www.kissmetrics.com/
[7.] https://www.woopra.com/
[8.] https://metrica.yandex.com/

Heatmapping and Session Recording Tools

There are blurred lines between the different types of analytics tools. Often tools will fall into more than one category and cover a range of services. The tools below focus primarily on heatmapping. Heatmapping covers a range of different click, scroll and mouse movement reports.

Heatmapping tools use colors to show graphical representations—primarily of where users have clicked on a page. They're useful for giving an "at a glance" indication of which elements on a page have received the most clicks. The heatmap below shows where users have clicked on a page. (Reports of this type are also referred to as "click maps".)

1-5. A screenshot showing an example of a heatmap

Scroll reports are another type of heatmap, and are really useful for indicating what content is just not being seen: they track how far down your pages users are scrolling.

Crazy Egg

Crazy Egg[9] works by taking a screenshot from a specified URL (or a collection of URLs), collecting all the clicks on that page, and projecting it as a heatmap on top of the screenshot. A lot of valuable data—such as the referrer, country, device type, etc.—are added to that click data. Heatmaps can be set up for specific device types, so you can see separate heatmaps for mobile, tablet and desktop users.

Scroll mapping is also available in Crazy Egg. Scroll maps can be used to show how much time users spend looking at sections of your page while they scroll.

Pros

Crazy Egg is very easy to set up on your website. All you have to do is insert a simple asynchronous script in the footer of the pages you want to track.

As touched on in the introduction, there are several different types of heatmap available within Crazy Egg, which means it can give you a lot of insight.

It's a very widely used tool as well, so there's plenty of support available for it. Crazy Egg also integrates with A/B testing tools like Optimizely. It works with HTTPS, iframes and Flash objects, making it particularly versatile.

Cons

A new "snapshot" needs to be set up for every page that you wish to analyze. Only when this has been set up can the data start to be recorded. This means that you won't have the same instant access to data as you can get with some of the other tools.

Crazy Egg only focuses on heatmapping. It offers in-depth heatmaps, but doesn't offer any other functionality. This may be a good thing, as it can focus on one area and provide a great heatmapping service. If you want session recording and form analytics, though, you may want to try another tool instead.

---

9. https://www.crazyegg.com/

Hotjar

Hotjar[10] offers a range of different tools. Heatmapping is one of these. You and can also see form analytics and session cam recordings of your users. Hotjar is a relative newcomer to the analytics market, having come out of beta in 2015.

Pros

As with a lot of analytics tools, Hotjar is easy to set up by just adding a line of code to your pages.

It's a bit of an "analytics Swiss army knife", as it includes heatmaps, session recordings, form analytics and several other tools. Despite this, it's a relatively inexpensive option compared with similar enterprise-level tools.

Hotjar can be used on multiple websites, making it a good option for agencies likely to want to analyze several different sites.

It also integrates with A/B testing tools, which is particularly cool for seeing the heatmaps, session recordings, and survey responses from audiences who saw different test variations.

Cons

Hotjar can be reliant on sampling data, which can lead to questionable data. Like Crazy Egg, it's not "always on", meaning that you have to manually set up tracking on individual pages.

The fact that Hotjar includes so many different tools means it can be overwhelming. It may also lead you to try to do too much and potentially waste valuable time over analyzing—though this isn't a fault of the tool!

Being a jack of all trades, it doesn't offer the level of targeting and analysis for each of the features that you're likely to get from more focused tools.

---

10. https://www.hotjar.com/

Clicktale

Clicktale[11] is a similar tool to Hotjar. It's described as a "customer experience analytics tool". Serving over 2,000 customers worldwide, including Fortune 500 businesses, Clicktale is one of the fastest-growing companies in this space.

Pros

Clicktale is an enterprise-level tool designed for larger websites. The tool is "always on", meaning that it continually pulls in data for every page it's set up on.

Clicktale has an even wider range of tools than Hotjar, giving an extremely detailed account of all user behavior.

Cons

As with Hotjar, there's a risk that Clicktale could provide more options that you need to analyze.

Cost could also be a barrier, as Clicktale is an enterprise-level tool with an enterprise-level subscription fee.

Other Notable Heatmapping Tools

There are lots of tools on the market that can provide you with heatmaps, session recordings and other analytics services.

Some of the more popular ones include Lucky Orange[12], Clicky[13], SessionCam[14], Inspectlet[15] and Mousestats[16]. Having used all of these (or at least

---

11. https://www.clicktale.com/
12. http://www.luckyorange.com/
13. https://clicky.com/
14. https://sessioncam.com/
15. http://www.inspectlet.com/
16. https://www.mousestats.com/

had demos of them), I've noticed a lot of similarities, making it hard to recommend any one individual tool.

Before you decide which heatmapping tool to use, you should first think about what you'd like it to do. Some tools have some great-sounding features, but you need to consider how often you would use them, and whether they would help or slow down your analysis process.

Split Testing Tools

Split testing is a method of conducting controlled, randomized experiments on two or more variations of a design, to see which variation generates the highest number of conversions. We'll cover split testing in detail in Chapter 6, but the section below gives a brief overview of some of the market-leading tools.

Optimizely

Optimizely[17] is an advanced split testing platform that's easy for beginners to get to grips with. The setup just requires the addition of a small code snippet to your pages, after which you're ready to set up your first split test. Customers are able to set up tests using a WYSIWYG editor or a code editor, depending on how comfortable they are with developing their own tests.

A 30-day free trial is available to everybody, so anyone can give the tool a try to see the functionality it offers.

The platform allows you to integrate with several other tools such as Google Analytics, Adobe Analytics and Crazy Egg.

Optimizely isn't the cheapest tool available, but it's one of the most popular due to its ease of use, advanced features and great support and community.

[17.] https://www.optimizely.com/

Adobe Target

Adobe's split testing tool Target[18] offers similar functionality to Optimizely. The tool is less accessible, as no free trial is available. It offers a strong enterprise-level solution, however, and integrates seamlessly with other Adobe Marketing Suite products. This makes creating audiences for tests, and analyzing results, easy for companies that are already using the other Adobe Marketing Suite tools.

Visual Website Optimizer (VWO)

VWO[19] is one of the most affordable split testing tools currently on the market. While low prices make the tool attractive to smaller companies, VWO is also used by leading brands like Microsoft, Virgin Holidays and Toyota. It's easy to use for both developers and non-developers, meaning there's a low barrier to getting tests set up.

The platform makes use of several built-in features, including a heatmapping tool that's available for all experiments.

Google Optimize 360

As a new-comer to the market, Google's Optimize 360[20] tool has a lot of catching up to do. The platform focuses on its native integration with Google Analytics. This provides you with the behavioral insights you need to create effective tests and to deliver optimized customer experiences.

The tool is easy to use, and its integration with Google Analytics means it's simple to set up, run and report on data-driven tests.

Other Useful Analytics Tools

This final section covers other types of analytics tools that can be useful for the UX process. New tools are being developed constantly, though, so don't be surprised to see new contenders emerging.

[18.] https://www.adobe.io/products/target
[19.] https://vwo.com/
[20.] https://www.google.com/analytics/optimize/

Usability Hub

UsabilityHub[21] offers a range of different tools to help you make design decisions. There are five different testing tools available: five second test, click test, question test, navigation test and preference test. These tests provide a mixture of qualitative and quantitative data. The quantitative tests are the click, navigation and preference tests.

Click tests work in a similar way to heatmapping tools. Users are asked to click on a screenshot rather than a fully functioning webpage. They're asked a question to begin with—such as "Where would you click to get in contact with us?"—and their responses are recorded on a heatmap. This test also times the average response, to show how quickly users were able to find your information.

Navigation tests work in a similar fashion, but they use multiple screenshots instead of one. Users are given multi-step tasks to follow, and clicking on the first screenshot will navigate them to a second, and so on.

Finally, the preference test is a simple way of finding out which design users prefer. You can upload two images, often screenshots, and ask users which they prefer. This gives simple, direct, quantitative feedback—though keep in mind that asking users what they want is not always the best option!

Formisimo

Formisimo[22] is a form and checkout analysis tool. It gives powerful data on how users are engaging with forms on your website. Users' actions are recorded on all form pages, showing which fields are causing problems. Formisimo records where users drop out of the form-filling process, and also which fields are taking users the longest to complete.

Because Formisimo only analyzes form usage, it's simple to use but gives vital, focused data. If your website analytics suggests that forms may be causing you an issue, a tool like Formisimo will give you more detailed data to analyze, better helping you to pinpoint the problem.

[21.] https://usabilityhub.com/
[22.] http://www.formisimo.com/

Woopra

Woopra[23] is a real-time customer analytics service that can track how individuals use your website or app. It tracks your new and unidentified website and mobile app users from their first touch anonymously, in a similar way to how the User Explorer reports in Google Analytics. Once the user chooses to sign up, subscribe or do something similar, all of their previous anonymous activity is merged into the same, identifiable customer profile. These customer profiles can contain all the information you have about a user, including details such as their name, company and email address.

Woopra is primarily used by marketing and sales teams, but it provides data that can be really useful for making UX decisions. It can help you understand user interaction on a deeper level than other analytics tools.

Using Tools Together

The tools covered in the previous section will all give you data about your user behavior. It's rare that any one tool will provide you with all of the data that you need. Combining data from different tools will give you more insight than focusing on data from a single source.

For example, you may start off by using a website analytics tool like Google Analytics to find out where problems are occurring on your site. This might identify a page, or group of pages, where you're seeing some worrying trends. You can then delve deeper into the problem using a heatmapping or form analytics tool to get a more precise idea of what specifically is causing the problem.

Some tools can be integrated, too. A good example of this is integrating your split testing platform with your website analytics. Your split test results will give you information on conversion performance, while your analytics will enable you to go deeper into the data and look at broader user behavior for the variations in your tests.

---

23. https://www.woopra.com/

Analytics Tools Summary

With so many different tools on the market, you could be forgiven for feeling a bit overwhelmed by the options. However, most of these tools do similar things and operate in a similar fashion, so if you're familiar with one tool, it shouldn't be too difficult to get to grips with another.

This book will primarily use examples from Google Analytics. That's because it's the most popular tool, it's free, and it's easy to set up, so there's no barrier to entry. It's important to remember, though, that the principles are more important than the tool itself. This book isn't a how-to guide or a textbook. Instead, it focuses on the best approaches to using analytics data in the UX process.

You may not have a choice of which analytics tool you use, but the tool is not as important as the technique. This book will arm you with the analytics knowledge you need to take your UX work to the next level.

Chapter 2

Getting Set Up

> It is a capital mistake to theorize before one has data. Insensibly one
> begins to twist facts to suit theories, instead of theories to suit facts.
> — *Arthur Conan Doyle, Sherlock Holmes*

Getting things set up right before you begin analysis is critically important. If the data you're analyzing is incorrect or incomplete, you'll risk coming to incorrect conclusions and wasting time fixing problems that aren't there. You might also act on false positives—for example, replicating something that looks to be working well, but actually isn't.

You'll also need to be confident in the data. As stated in the previous chapter, the data you get from your analytics package is "black and white", so you need to be sure the numbers are as accurate as possible. This isn't a matter of opinion; the numbers shouldn't lie.

Checking Your Setup

The first step in analyzing web analytics data is to get access to it. If you're working on behalf of a client, you'll need to ask them to add your email address to the list of users. For Google Analytics, this means getting you set up with user permissions for their analytics at an account, property or view level.

If there's no existing analytics account, this will need to be set up. As covered in the previous chapter, some web analytics tools are easier to set up than others. I recommend using Google Analytics if you're starting from scratch, as it's free, easy to use and easy to set up.

The following section looks at where to start if you're using Google Analytics. If you're using another platform, such as Adobe Analytics, the access levels will differ.

Accounts, Properties and Views

Each Google account can be granted access to Google Analytics at an account, property or view level. It's important to understand the hierarchy of Google Analytics to ensure that you have access to the right reports.

Account

An **account** is the top level of the Google Analytics hierarchy. You need at least one account so you can have access to Analytics, and so you can identify the properties you want to track. You can have multiple different Analytics accounts. There will often (but not always) be one account for each website. If you work for an agency, it's likely you'll have one account per client.

Property

A **property** is normally a website or mobile application, and an account can contain one or more properties. Within your Analytics account, you can add the properties you want to collect data from. When you add a property to an account, Google Analytics generates the tracking code needed for collecting data from that property. Google Analytics will automatically create one view for each property you add, but you can create more yourself.

View

A **view** is the bottom level of the hierarchy, and is where you access your reports. You give users access to a view so they can see the reports based on that view's data. A property can contain one or more views. Views will generally all contain data from the same website, but filters can be applied to each view to change the data they include. A common example of this is where you filter out visits from your own IP address so that your visits to the website aren't counted in the reports.

Accounts, Properties & Views

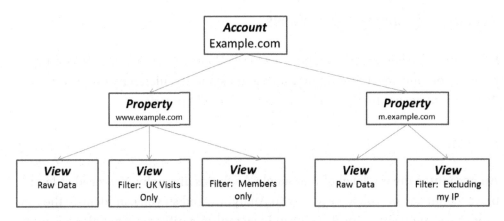

2-1. Google Analytics account structure

It's important to know which accounts, properties or views you're able to access. You may be set up with access to a view that filters out information that may be useful to you. Without knowledge of how the view has been set up, you won't know whether you're looking at all the data you want to see.

For example, if a website deals primarily with a UK audience, a view for that website may be set up to include only UK visitors. If you're not aware of this from the beginning, it may mean the data you see doesn't give a true reflection of all website visitors.

If you're setting up your own views, it's important to keep one "raw" view that includes all visitor information. This will act as a backup in case you make an error when setting up additional views.

Once you have a raw view, you'll probably want to set up one main "reporting" view. This should filter out visits from your IP address, as well as the IP address of your client if you're working on behalf of someone else. You can have up to 25 views per property, though I wouldn't recommend using anywhere near this amount, as things will begin to get complicated and messy!

Other analytics packages will have similar hierarchical structures. It's important that you know the context of any reports you're looking at, so try to find out as much as you can about the overall Analytics setup.

Getting Access to Analytics

Now that you have an understanding of accounts, properties and views, you'll be able to request access to a client's Google Analytics account. You don't need a Google account to be able to do this.

There are four different levels of access for Google Analytics:

- **Manage users**. This is the highest permission level. Managers can manage existing account permissions and set up new accounts. However, they cannot edit accounts.
- **Edit**. Editors can perform administrative and report-related functions, but not create accounts. This level of access is required for making changes to the overall Analytics setup.
- **Collaborate**. Collaborators can create their own personal assets, such as custom reports, and share them. They cannot make major changes to the overall setup.
- **Read & Analyze**. Users with this permission level can see report and configuration data. They cannot collaborate on shared assets.

In short, if you're planning to make changes to the Analytics setup, you'll need to request Edit permissions. This will enable you to set up filters, goals and other important features.

Other analytics tools will likely have similar permission types. Have a chat with the person in charge of the analytics account to find out what level of access they're willing to give you.

Before you dive right into the reports, there are a few key areas that you'll want to check relating to your Analytics setup.

Analytics Checklist

While it's tempting to start looking at analytics reports straight away, it pays to spend some initial time outside of the reports to ensure that you understand, and are happy with, the general setup. The following areas should be checked to make sure everything's in order.

Is the Analytics Code Installed on Every Page?

The analytics tracking code needs to be on every page of a website, or every "screen" in an app. This ensures that visitor information is recorded for every page so you're not missing out on any data. Perhaps more importantly, though, it also ensures that visits are recorded continuously. If the code is missing from a page, a user will appear to leave the website when they visit that page, and will appear to visit again after moving to another page that does have the tracking code.

There are various tools for checking whether the tracking code is installed site-wide. One of the simplest and easiest to use if you're checking your Google Analytics setup is GA Checker[1]. This will scan your entire website (as long as it's no more than 10,000 pages) and will tell you which pages contain the tracking code and which don't.

Is the Analytics Code Installed in the Correct Place?

A fairly common issue with the installation of analytics tools is that the code is added to the wrong place on the page. The optimal placement of the tracking code may vary for different analytics tools, but for Google Analytics it's best

---

[1.] http://www.gachecker.com

placed just before the closing `</head>` tag of each page. It will work if placed further down a page, but including it at the bottom of a page might not count people that land on the page, stay for a short period of time and then leave.

If you're using Google Tag Manager, or another tag management tool, you can add the tracking code through this. Tag management tools are essentially content management systems for snippets of code, such as analytics tracking code. If you don't have access to the tag management tool being used on your website, you may need to request access to check that everything has been set up correctly.

Are Custom "Events" Set Up?

Analytics packages track web page views. Normally, the code snippet fires when a user visits a page, and the analytics package records that visit, as well as details such as the visitor's location, the device they're using, and whether or not they're a first-time visitor. What web analytics tools *don't* generally tell you by default is where users are clicking within that web page.

Users can do a lot on a website even if they only visit a single page. They might play a video, or engage in "live chat" with a customer service representative. By default, your analytics package is unlikely to track this kind of activity. Analytics packages also won't track views of PDF files. This means that, for one-page websites, the out-of-the-box analytics reports will be almost useless!

To track engagement within pages using Google Analytics, you'll need to use **event tracking**. This involves measuring user clicks rather than visits to different pages. If you have a PDF file that people can download from your website, you'll need to add event tracking code within the link to the file. Then, every time a user clicks on that link, that click will be recorded in your Google Analytics reports.

To find the events reports in Google Analytics, you'll need to visit **Behavior > Events**. We'll cover these reports in more detail later on, but at this stage you should just have a quick look at those reports to see what's been set up and consider if that data will be useful for you, and if any other events need to be set up.

Are Custom "Goals" Set Up?

By default, analytics packages will record a lot of information about visits to your website. Any good analytics tool will show you details such as how many visits you had, which pages your users viewed, how long they stayed and so on. But without some customization, no tool will be able to show you information about your website "goals"—unless those goals are particularly simple.

In analytics terms, a **goal** is a notable action taken by a user on your website or app. This will obviously vary on different types of websites, but the following are all examples of goals:

- completing a contact form
- calling a phone number on the website (requires call tracking)
- downloading a brochure
- registering for an account
- requesting a demo of a service
- subscribing to a newsletter
- booking an appointment
- registering for a (free) event
- social shares
- comments
- customer reviews
- engagement with live chat
- playing a video

You'll notice that none of the examples above involve making a purchase. That's because analytics packages will normally treat ecommerce data differently from goal data, often providing separate ecommerce reports. We'll cover ecommerce set up in the "Is Ecommerce Tracking Set Up?" section below.

There's no way for your analytics to know which goals are relevant to your website, so you'll need to check if these have been set up already. If they haven't been set up, you may have to set them up yourself.

The first step here is to decide which goals you'd like to track. To do this, you need to consider the objective of the website, and what actions users can take to help achieve that objective. For example, if you're analyzing the website of a web design agency, you might be looking for potential clients to get in touch. In this scenario, the primary goal is likely to be your contact form, or making a phone enquiry. You may also want to set up goals for users subscribing to your newsletter and downloading resources.

Once you have an idea of what your goals should be, you can check if they've already been set up. You'll also want to double check that they've been set up correctly. Just because a goal is present doesn't mean it's tracking as it should be.

In Google Analytics, goal information can be found in **Conversions > Goals > Overview**.

Another aspect of the goal setup you'll want to check is whether goal funnels have been configured. **Goal funnels** are a way of analyzing the user journey for goals that have multiple steps. An example of this might be a registration form that's split over two or more pages. If a goal funnel is set up, you'll be able to see the dropout rate at each step. The screenshot below shows a goal funnel for the registration process of a website:

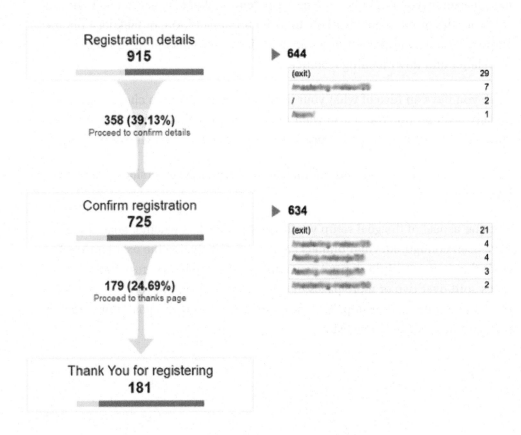

2-2. An analytics funnel diagram

The labeled boxes represent pages in the process. The arrows between them represent people moving to the next step of the funnel. These are labeled with the percentage of people who moved to the next step. The red arrows to the side of these show how many people dropped out at each step, and whether they exited the website completely or went on to visit another page outside of the funnel.

To check if funnels have been set up in Google Analytics, you'll need to visit **Conversions > Goals > Funnel Visualization**.

From here, you'll need to select the appropriate goal from the drop-down options on the top left of the report page.

If funnels haven't been set up, you can set them up yourself [2], though they won't work retrospectively.

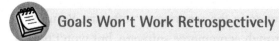

Goals Won't Work Retrospectively

If you set up a goal today, it will only start tracking from today, but it can't be applied to any of your past data.

We'll cover how goal data can be used in your analysis later on. At this stage, it's important just to know what's been set up, and to think about whether additional goals need to be set up.

Is Ecommerce Tracking Set Up?

If you're analyzing an ecommerce website, one of the most important factors is likely to be the money that users are spending when on the site. Ecommerce tracking is also not set up by default, and needs to be set up by adding tracking code to the purchase confirmation page of your checkout.

To find out if ecommerce tracking has been set up in Google Analytics for your website, you'll need to check the **Conversions > Ecommerce > Overview** report. If you're seeing data there, then ecommerce reporting has been set up. This means you'll be able to see figures like conversion rate and average order value.

Ecommerce reports won't exactly match the data you see from your shopping cart software. This is because not everyone is tracked by Google Analytics, and is also due to incomplete or test orders. Some possible reasons for this are:

- **Some users are not being tracked by Google Analytics**. Users may have JavaScript or cookies disabled. You should also be aware that some ad-blocking tools block analytics tracking by default.
- **JavaScript tracking setup issues**. For example, amounts that contain commas can cause JavaScript issues if the ecommerce tracking is not set up correctly. There can also be problems caused by leaving form fields blank and using curly quotes (' ') instead of straight quotes (' ') in your JavaScript.
- **Duplicate transactions**. Users may refresh confirmation pages, leading to duplication of the same transaction in Google Analytics. This will inflate the revenue figures.

[2.] If you'd like some guidance, http://www.lukehay.co.uk/2016/12/funnels-google-analytics/ covers the basics of goal funnel setup

- **Post-purchase changes have been made in the ecommerce software**. Refunds or order alterations can be made through ecommerce software, but won't be replicated in your analytics tool. It's now possible to upload details of your refunds to Google Analytics, which will help minimize the differences between your Analytics figures and those from your ecommerce software. This does require manual intervention, though.

If the difference between your Analytics data and your cart data is greater than 10% you should investigate further. A discrepancy this large suggest there's something wrong with your setup. 10% is a figure quoted by Google itself, though if you want to be particularly cautious, you may want to look into potential issues if the difference is more than 5%.

Potential ecommerce tracking issues should be investigated by running a number of test transactions with a debugger like Fiddler[3] to ensure the right data is sent to Google Analytics every time.

Is Internal Site Search Set Up?

If your website uses search functionality, this can give you some very useful data about user intent. By default, your analytics package won't track internal site search usage. If internal site search isn't already set up, you'll want to set it up yourself to begin collecting this search data.

We'll cover how to analyze this data later, but to check if site search has been set up in Google Analytics, you'll need to go to **Behavior > Site Search > Overview**. If you see data there, this feature has already been set up.

Have Demographic Reports Been Enabled?

Google Analytics can now provide demographics data on your website visitors. This information is collected based on the websites your users have visited. Google tries to predict your users' gender and age. This is similar to techniques that have been used by traditional media for years. As well as browsing behavior, Google also uses data that your users have provided themselves, such as information they've given on social networking websites.

[3.] http://www.telerik.com/fiddler

This demographic information can be really useful for your user research process, and can give you real insight into how different user groups interact with your site. However, these reports aren't set up by default. The following screenshot shows an example of these reports:

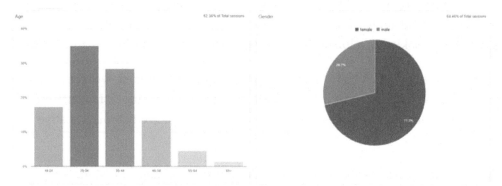

2-3. Demographic reports in Google Analytics

To view these reports in Google Analytics, visit **Audience > Demographics > Overview**. If you see data there, the demographics reports have been enabled. If you see a message giving you the option to enable the reports, you'll need to do the following:

- ensure that **Enable Demographics** and **Interests Reports** are to set to "on" in your property settings
- agree to Google's policy requirements for **Advertising Features**
- click the **Enable** button on the reports.

Once this has been completed, you should start to see demographic information appearing within 24 hours. We'll look at how this data can be analyzed later on in this book, but it's important that you set this up quickly if it hasn't already been set up for your account. The sooner you enable demographics reports, the sooner you can begin collecting this useful data.

This data can be a really useful addition to your user research, but we'll cover that in more detail in Chapter 5.

How Much Data Do You Have Available?

When it comes to analyzing your data, you'll normally want to make sure you're looking over a long time period to begin with. Most of the time, recent data will only tell you part of the story. There will be exceptions to this, such as looking at the data for a particular day, but to get a good idea of how a website is performing, looking at a longer time period provides more useful insights.

Most websites are affected by seasonal factors. Many ecommerce websites see a lot more activity in the run-up to the holiday season, for example. In contrast, business-to-business websites tend to see a decrease in activity around festive periods.

When getting access to an analytics account for the first time, one of the first things I do is check how many months and years of data I have at my disposal. Looking back over previous years enables me to understand the history of a website. Comparing different years' worth of data enables me to get a good understanding of the seasonal patterns, and also tells me whether the website's performance has been improving or going backwards over time.

However, validating the accuracy of previously collected data is difficult. For example, tracking could have been set up incorrectly a year ago and only have been fixed recently. It's worth speaking with the person who's been managing the analytics account to find out if there are any potential issues with the data you should be aware of.

To check how much data you've got to play with, you'll need to use the date picker to look back over time. Select an early date (for example, ten years ago) as your start date, and then you'll be able to see on the overview graph when data was first collected.

2-4. Changing reporting dates in Google Analytics

Once you know how much data you have, you'll be able to compare data over time. To do this, select the time period you want to begin with and then tick the **Compare to** box.

You can then compare to either the previous period, the previous year, or a custom date range.

Be Wary of Data Sampling

One thing to be wary of when looking at a lot of data over a long period of time is the possibility that your analytics package is sampling the data.

Sampling can be an issue when you're analyzing large amounts of data. Sampling is the process of selecting a subset of traffic data and reporting on the trends detected in that subset. Sampled data is a representation of some of your traffic; it's not a complete traffic data set. If your reports are sampled, they won't be as accurate as those that include all data.

Data sampling is not really an issue if the sample is based on a very high percentage (90%+) of the total traffic. You'll need to be aware that these are not precise numbers, but they'll generally be good enough for most types of analysis.

However, if the sample is based on a smaller percentage of the traffic, it can be very misleading. Looking at the behavior of less than 10% of users, and assuming that this is representative of all users, is likely to lead to inaccurate conclusions.

Sampling can be reduced in some analytics tools. In Google Analytics, you'll sometimes be presented with a slider that allows you to get higher precision, but with a slower load time for your reports.

If you start seeing warning messages about sampling on your reports, you'll want to reduce the reporting period you're looking at to remove the sampling.

Does Your Analytics Data Match Other Data Sources?

It's a good idea to cross check your analytics data against other sources to see whether there are any big discrepancies. You might want to compare your analytics figures to log files, sales figures or other analytics packages to see if they roughly match or if they're massively off. Otherwise, there's really no way to know if what you're seeing is correct.

It's rare that this type of data from different sources will be exactly the same, but if you see big discrepancies, you'll want to investigate further to see if you can spot any issues with the setup. This type of comparative analysis should reassure you that your data is accurate, enabling you to analyze with confidence.

Is Your Analytics Account Well Annotated?

It's likely that you'll spot several spikes and dips in website activity if you're looking at data over a long period of time. If you haven't been involved with the website for long, you may struggle to work out what's caused the irregular activity. Even if you have been working on the website for a long time, you may not remember exactly what happened two years ago to cause that big spike. This is where annotations come in handy.

In Google Analytics, **annotations** are found below the graphs that appear on most overview reports. As shown in the screenshot below, annotations are represented by a small comment style icon:

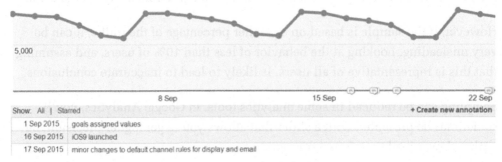

2-5. Annotations in Google Analytics

To add an annotation, you can click on the **Create new annotation** link and enter the details of what change occurred on that date. It's a good idea to include hyperlinks in your annotations that link to more information. This could be a longer-form note, or a link to the Internet Archive's Wayback Machine[4] showing what the website looked like before the change was made. Annotations in Google Analytics are limited to just 160 characters, so if you need to go into more detail, then link out to another source.

Before you start analyzing the data, you'll want to have a quick read of the existing annotations, so you're aware of any major changes that occurred and which may have impacted on the performance of the website. This will give some context to your analysis, and will help you begin to understand a little of the *why* as well as the *what*.

It's likely that the analytics data you're looking at will contain few or even no annotations. Annotations rely on analysts manually adding them, so they won't be thorough for all analytics accounts. Fortunately, annotations can be added retrospectively. This means that, if you can find out anecdotally when major website changes occurred, you can then go back and add annotations into Google Analytics. These will be highly beneficial when it comes to analyzing the data in the future.

 When to Add Annotations

> I recommend adding annotations whenever a change is made to tracking, whenever there's a big change Google Analytics or when something major changes on the website, or in the wider industry.

Has Content Grouping Been Set Up?

Analytics packages will tell you which pages of your website users have visited. This is great for UX work, as you can use this information to find out how individual pages are performing, and then make improvements based on underperforming pages. We'll cover the best way to do this later in the book.

---

[4] http://archive.org/web/

When analyzing pages, it's not always practical to evaluate single pages on their own. This may be because a website has thousands of pages, making analyzing each one of them almost impossible! It's also likely that page templates are used on the website, meaning that it may make more sense to analyze all of the pages that use a particular template together. For example, if you're dealing with an ecommerce site, it may make sense to group all product pages together, rather than look at thousands of individual product pages. This is where content grouping in Google Analytics comes in handy.

Content grouping is essentially a way to segment your data by the types of pages users visit on your site. As the name suggests, it gives you a way to group your content in a variety of ways. A simple example would be to group all of your blog posts separately from the rest of your site. If you have an ecommerce site, you might want to group your pages into categories. You might want to create a group for all product pages, and one for all the pages in your checkout process. How you group your pages will depend on the type of website you're working with.

Content grouping is also particularly useful if your site doesn't have an easy way to identify a template from its URL. For example, if product pages have an SKU number in the URL, you can often use a regex to filter reports just for product pages.

To check if content grouping has been set up, you'll need to go to **Behavior > Site Content > All Pages** to get to the main pages report. From here, you'll see a drop-down labeled as **Content Grouping** if this has been set up:

Page Types (Content Group) ⑦	Page views	que Views 1 (Page Types) ⑦	Avg. Time on Page ⑦
	1,110,144 % of Total: 100.00% (1,110,144)	408,495 % of Total: 100.00% (408,495)	00:01:06 Avg for View: 00:01:06 (0.00%)
1. Search Results Pages	461,044 (41.53%)	102,360 (25.06%)	00:00:46
2. Property View Pages	348,024 (31.35%)	127,028 (31.10%)	00:01:45
3. Home page	60,743 (5.47%)	47,638 (11.66%)	00:00:53

2-6. Content Grouping in Google Analytics

We'll cover how to analyze grouped content in the next chapter. At this stage, you'll want to check if it's been set up, and if you find it hasn't been set up already, you may want to set it up yourself[5].

Common Pitfalls to Avoid

When you first start analyzing data, it's easy to make mistakes, particularly if you're new to analytics. Don't let that put you off, though! This section lists some of the main pitfalls, and how they're best avoided—to ensure your analysis paints a true picture of user behavior.

Confusing Visits and Views

Different analytics tools will use different terminology to describe the same thing. For rookie analysts, this can cause confusion, and can mean that the wrong data is reported. Even within the same tool, terminology can be confusing. One of the most common mistakes people make is to confuse visits and views.

A **visit** (now known as a **session** in Google Analytics) generally describes a group of interactions one user takes within a given time frame on your website. A **view** (or "pageview" in some tools) describes a view of a page on your site that is tracked by the analytics tracking code.

These are two entirely different things, but visits and views are sometimes used interchangeably when people talk about their analytics. As you can imagine, this can cause problems for analysts, as reports will become inaccurate. Make sure you understand the terminology, so that you know what you're reporting on. (See the Google Analytics glossary at the end of this book if you're unsure.)

Obsessing over Visits and Views

When it comes to analyzing your data, you need to make sure you're analyzing the most important areas. A very common mistake people make is to focus purely on visits and views. Because you're a UXer, I know I don't need to convince you

---

[5.] Instructions for setting up content grouping can be found here:
http://www.lukehay.co.uk/2016/12/google-analytics-content-grouping/

that there's more to a website than just a lot of people visiting it! You may still find yourself under pressure, though, to increase page views or even visits. Leave this side of things to marketers, and focus your efforts on the numbers that relate to user experience.

Getting Drawn into the Numbers

Quantitative data is all about numbers. If your account is set up correctly, the numbers don't lie! Despite this, you need to make sure you don't forget what the numbers actually represent: real users.

As stated previously, the numbers will tell you what happened, not why, and this is why it's important not to forget to ask why. You'll need to look beyond the numbers and consider their context. Make sure you don't fall into the trap of just reporting what has happened: be sure to consider the bigger picture and think about what the numbers mean for the user experience of your website.

This is where you'll need to bring in the qualitative methods we touched on previously. You can often use analytics to find a problem, and user research methods to solve it.

Thinking Low Numbers Are Always Bad

One side effect of getting drawn into the numbers is that you automatically consider low numbers, or a drop in numbers, to be bad. While a drop in purchases is likely to be a bad thing, a reduction in the time users spend on particular pages, for example, could be good *or* bad.

If you've redesigned the home page on a website and the time people are spending on it drops, this could be due to the improved efficiency of your design. It may be that people are able to navigate more quickly to areas of interest to them. Once again, context is key here. Work out what any drops actually mean for the website as a whole, rather than assuming they're always going to be negative.

Confusing Correlation with Causation

Just because something happens to your analytics at the same time as you make a change to the website doesn't mean the two are connected. If you notice changes to your analytics after making a change, you need to be sure it's not a coincidence and that the two are connected.

You're likely to have to delve a little deeper into your reports to prove that the rise in conversion rate was due to your great new design. This is covered in more detail in Chapter 6, but it's something you should be aware of before you take credit (or blame!) for any sizable shifts in your reporting data.

The graph below, taken from tylervigen.com[6], shows a correlation of close to 95% for cheese consumption and number of people who died by becoming tangled in their bed sheets:

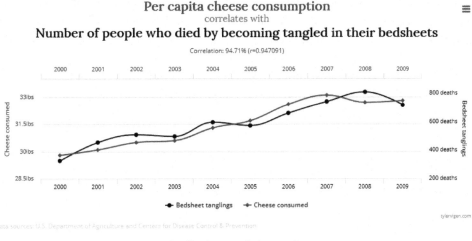

2-7. Spurious correlations graph

There's also a strong correlation between ice cream sales and drownings at sea, as both go up in the summer. Only an analyst severely lacking common sense would say that ice cream causes drowning, though!

The correlation versus causation issue is probably the most prolific mistake I see people make when analyzing data. When it comes to website analytics, one

---

[6.] http://tylervigen.com/spurious-correlations

example of this might be where data shows that people who use site search covert 50% more than those who don't. This could convince UXers to encourage more people to use the site search. However, the more likely correlation is that people who use the site search are a more engaged audience than the average users, and also have a better idea of what they're looking for—meaning that they naturally have higher conversion rates.

Combining quant and qual (and sometimes your own common sense) will help ensure you don't fall into the trap of confusing correlation and causation. Split testing is also a great way to determine true causation, and will help to protect against drawing incorrect conclusions from your data. We'll cover split testing more in Chapter 6.

Grouping All Visits Together

As UXers, we know that different people use websites in different ways. We also know that the same person is likely to use a website differently when using different devices, or even using the same website at different times of the day. We need to include these considerations of user behavior in our quantitative analysis.

If a website has a conversion rate of 5%, this tells us one story. If we break that figure down, though, and see that the conversion rate is 10% for desktop users and only 1% for mobile users, that tells a different story, and gives a good indication of where we should focus our UX efforts!

Segmenting users is key to understanding how a website is performing. We'll cover segmentation in more detail later in Chapter 3.

Analyzing Too Broadly

With a wealth of data available, knowing where to start analyzing it all can be difficult. When starting a new project, you might want to have a quick, top-level assessment of the available data. But useful insight comes from digging deeper.

Looking at "headline" figures may give an overall indication of a website's current performance, but it's unlikely to give the information we need to improve the UX. Where possible, it's best to approach your analytics with a goal in mind. This will help focus your efforts, and should help you avoid feeling overwhelmed by the sheer amount of data available. The chapters of this book relate to current UX goals, and are designed to help you approach data analysis in the right way.

The number of visits (or "sessions") a website receives is often a figure that people focus in on. This metric tells us little about a website's performance, though, as the purpose of most websites is to do more than just act as a destination for users. It's far more important to know how users are engaging with individual pages, and how many of those pages are converting. I'd much rather have a website with 1,000 visitors a month and a conversion rate of 10% than a website with 5,000 visitors a month and a conversion rate of 1%, wouldn't you?

Focusing on Numbers Rather than Trends

It can be tempting to look at numbers and make a judgement about whether they're "good" or "bad". One question I often get asked during my training sessions is "What's a good average visit duration?" There isn't a simple answer to this question. It will depend on your website and what you're trying to achieve. What's seen as good for one website might be seen as terrible for another.

It's important to look at whether your key metrics are increasing or decreasing over time. You might also want to set targets to give yourself something to aim for. Just looking at recent figures in isolation tells you very little. In short, don't worry so much about the numbers; worry more about whether they're going up or down, and how that relates to the UX goals you've set.

Remember, though: it's all about context. Big increases or drops in metrics, or particularly high or low metrics, need to be considered in relation to what's happening elsewhere on the website or app. For example, if product-page views dropped by 2% over three months, you may not think much of it, but if all other pages had an increase in views of 30% over the same period, suddenly this 2% drop looks like something worth investigating.

Including Bot or Spam Traffic

Certain types of traffic can skew your analytics data if you're not careful. You only want to record visits from real users, and not artificial "bot" traffic.

Search engines use bots to crawl websites and index the web so they can return relevant search results to users. Bots used by all the major search engines don't show up in most analytics tools, and you wouldn't want to block these bots from crawling your website. You do, however, want to block bots that artificially inflate your analytics numbers.

The amount of bots that execute JavaScript is steadily increasing. Bots now frequently view more than just one page on your website, and some of them even convert on your analytics goals. As bots become smarter, you also need to become smarter, to ensure this traffic doesn't cloud your judgement when you make important business decisions based on the data in your analytics platform.

The Fresh Egg blog provides a useful guide on how to spot, and block, spam traffic from your analytics tool in its article "How to Deal With Bot Traffic in Your Google Analytics"[7].

Not Customizing Your Setup

Standard reports in some analytics tools can be really detailed and will provide you with a lot of useful information. But, as mentioned earlier, the standard reporting setup will only get you so far. Each website works differently, so don't take a one-size-fits-all approach to your analytics. Instead, customize your setup to make sure you get the data you need.

Not Generating Actionable Takeaways

You can get a lot of information from your analytics package, and you can present this as important-looking reports and really impress people. What's more important, however, is coming away from your analysis with actionable next steps based on the data.

Spotting trends and uncovering potential problems is only doing half the job! If you notice that tablet users are viewing considerably fewer pages than their desktop counterparts, what does this mean? What are you proposing to do about it? While you won't get an answer about how to fix a problem from your

---

[7.] http://www.freshegg.co.uk/blog/analytics/how-to-deal-with-bot-traffic-in-your-google-analytics

analytics, you should be able to propose your next step. Perhaps the fact that tablet users are seemingly less engaged than desktop users will lead you to do some usability testing on tablets? Or maybe you think you should do additional user research to find out the context in which your tablet users are visiting your website? Whatever you decide, it's important that you do decide to do something. Analyzing the numbers is just the start; make sure you follow that up with action!

Your analytics data can also help you prioritize those next steps, as it can help quantify the volume of lost visitors, or sales, or something else, caused by each issue you've spotted.

What Next?

Once your analytics package is set up correctly, and you know what data you have available, you can begin to analyze it. The next chapter looks at some common analytics terms, gives a guide to the Google Analytics interface, and provides tips on how to go about really scrutinizing your data.

Chapter **3**

An Introduction to Analyzing Data

If you can't explain it simply, you don't understand it well enough.
— *Albert Einstein, Physicist*

Once your analytics tool is set up to collect data correctly, you can begin to analyze the data. This chapter will give some tips for data analysis, and will introduce some of the key terms used by Google Analytics and other website analytics tools.

Key Analytics Terms

For those not used to looking at website analytics, some of the terminology can seem like a foreign language. This can get even more confusing when terms change, or when different tools use different terms to describe the same thing.

Some analytics terms that are used regularly are often misunderstood. In some cases, a partial understanding of a term may be more dangerous than having no understanding at all. One commonly misunderstood example is the word "hit".

A **hit** is often thought of as being a synonym for a page view or a visit. This is not the case, as each file request to a web server is an individual hit.

This means that, if a web page contains five images, a user viewing this page will count as one page view *but six hits* (the five images plus the HTML page itself). You can see how this misunderstanding can lead to a wildly inaccurate understanding of the data! This section covers the most important analytics terms. (There are also short definitions of the main terms in the glossary at the end of this book.)

Dimensions and Metrics

All the data in your analytics reports can be divided into dimensions and metrics. It's important to know what each term means so that you can better analyze your data. A good understanding of dimensions and metrics is also important for setting up custom reports and dashboards.

Dimensions are a way to group data—a form of categorization or identification. A dimension does *not* refer to the *size* of something (a common misunderstanding). Dimensions are normally shown in the first column of your reports. Examples of dimensions include *Country*, *Page Title* and *Device Type*.

Metrics, on the other hand, are the numbers associated with those dimensions. They appear in the other columns of your reports, showing the numbers relating to the dimensions in the first column. Examples of metrics include *Pageviews*, *Bounce Rate* and *Avg. Time on Page*. Metrics help you understand the behavior of your users. They count how often things happen—such as the number of visits to your website or app. Metrics can be totals, averages or percentages of a total.

The screenshot below shows dimensions and metrics, as well as the different ways metrics are counted:

Dimension ↓		Metrics ⟶		
Page ⑦		**Pageviews** ⑦	↓ **Avg. Time on Page** ⑦	**Bounce Rate** ⑦
		23,958	**00:01:41**	**53.07%**
		% of Total: 100.00% (23,958)	Avg for View: 00:01:41 (0.00%)	Avg for View: 53.07% (0.00%)
1. /	⑤	4,343 (18.13%)	00:01:01	38.14%
2. /events/	⑤	3,918 (16.36%)	00:01:36	49.63%
3. /about/	⑤	1,309 (5.46%)	00:01:08	76.30%
4. /get-involved/	⑤	685 (2.86%)	00:01:15	71.79%

3-1. Dimensions and Metrics

An easy way to differentiate the two is to remember that dimensions are often words, while metrics are more likely to be numbers.

Sessions, Visits, Page Views and Unique Page Views

As touched on in the previous chapter, there is often confusion between sessions, visits and page views. Firstly, it's worth pointing out that sessions and visits are essentially the same thing. Google Analytics previously used the term "visit", but changed the terminology to "sessions" in 2014. Other tools, such as Adobe Analytics, still use the term "visits".

You'll generally find that the two terms are used interchangeably, but as long as you know these are referring to the same thing, it shouldn't be a problem.

A **session**, or visit, is a group of interactions (or a single interaction) that a user takes within a given time frame on your website. Google Analytics sessions time out after 30 minutes of inactivity by default, though you can change this yourself in your analytics settings.

This means that, if your user goes to make themself a coffee, leaving your website open in their browser, and returns within half an hour, this will be counted as the same session. The same can be said for users who hop between multiple tabs. More often than not, though, sessions represent continuous browsing of your website.

Sessions don't differentiate between unique individuals. They only count the number of sessions, regardless of who's doing them. If I visit your website in the morning and come back in the evening, that would still count as two sessions.

Using other metrics like *users* or *visitors* will give you information on about individuals who visit your website. The next section in this chapter covers users and visitors in detail.

Page views are simply views to an HTML page or, less commonly, virtual page views. A **virtual page view** is a way of telling Google Analytics to register a page view if a new HTML page has not been loaded. Virtual page views require additional tagging in the form of JavaScript code. You can use them everywhere where content is loaded without a reload of the page, or when two or more pieces of content can reside on the same URL—for example, a form submission, or one-page checkouts.

You can have multiple page views during one session if a user is browsing your website. Page views are normally categorized as page views and unique page views. If a user views the same page more than once during a session, this will only count as a single unique page view. This is useful if you want to get an idea of how many sessions included a view to a particular page, but you don't want that number inflated by users who returned to that page in the same session.

Users and Visitors

As Uxers, we have a good idea of what a "user" is. In our industry, users would generally be defined as individual humans who interact with our product—often a website, app or a piece of software. Analytics packages rarely have a way of accurately identifying individuals, though, so in analytics the term "user" has a slightly different meaning from the normal one.

Most of the major analytics tools will identify users based on cookies. If I visit your website from my laptop, your analytics tool will normally drop a cookie into my browser so that, when I return, it will recognize me as the same individual who visited previously.

This is broadly correct, but it doesn't take into account that I might share my laptop with someone else. This means that two different individuals can be counted as the same user. Conversely, analytics tools are often unable to identify cross-device (or cross-browser) visits. If I visit your website from my tablet, your analytics tool will be unlikely to identify me as the same user who visited from my laptop.

If you have a website that requires users to log in, or uses some other sort of unique identifier such as an email address or mobile number, then this may enable you to track users across devices. This requires additional setup, though, and relies on users logging in or otherwise identifying themselves on each of their devices.

As with sessions and visits, "users" and "visitors" are generally different terms for the same thing. Different tools will use different terminology, but as long as you remember that *visitors* and *users* both normally describe a theoretical individual, based on a cookie, then that'll be good enough.

Users, or visitors, are often broken down into "new" and "returning". New visitors are people who have visited your website for the first time during your reporting period, while returning visitors have visited more than once. By breaking this down, your analytics tool enables you to easily compare the behavior of these two user groups.

You need to be careful here, though, as the metrics "new" and "returning" may not be as accurate as you'd expect. As touched on previously, analytics packages rarely track cross-device visits. This means that, if I start something on my phone and finish it on my laptop, it's likely that I'll be recorded as a "new" user when I visit via my laptop. Also, users will be recorded as "new" if they clear their cookies, or have a JavaScript or ad blocker installed.

Visit/Session Duration and Time on Page

Time-based metrics are notoriously inaccurate. This is partly due to the way they're calculated, and partly due to the inability to track a user's attention.

Google Analytics calculates **session duration** as the time between the first and last interaction during a visit to your website. It does not, as you might expect, calculate the duration based on when the user arrives on your website and when they leave. Google Analytics has no way of knowing when a user exits your website; it can only track their interactions while they're on it. This means that, if a user spends five minutes looking at your home page, 20 minutes reading a blog post, and then exits the website, their visit duration was just five minutes. Conversely, if a user has left your website open in another tab for ten minutes while they browse another site, as long as they return to your site and move on to another web page, that ten minutes will count towards their duration on your site!

Time-on-page metrics work in a similar fashion to session duration. The timer starts when a user first loads a particular page and stops when they move on to another page on the website. No time is recorded for that page if a user exits your website from there. This means that a user can read a long blog post on your website, but if they exit from that point before viewing any other pages, their recorded "time on page" will be zero seconds. If a user only visits a single page during their session, both their time on that page and their session duration will be registered as zero seconds.

All of this means that time-based metrics are not very accurate at all.

This underlines the importance of analyzing based on trends over time, rather than looking at exact figures. If your average session duration is five minutes, that may not tell you very much. You're better off focusing on what the session duration was last month, or last year, and analyzing whether this has gone up or down—and, most importantly, finding out why.

You need to be careful here, though. If, for example, a blog post on your website gets lots of attention on social media one month, and drives lots of users who just read the post, then leave, this alone could massively impact your average session duration. This underlines the need to be aware of what's happening across all of your website, and to avoid focusing on the headline figures.

Bounce and Exit Rates

Two metrics that often get confused are bounce and exit rates. These are reported in slightly different ways in different analytics tools. The definitions below are based on how they're reported in Google Analytics.

A **bounce** describes a single page visit to a website. This means that the user arrives on a page and then leaves without viewing any other pages. The bounce rate is the percentage of visits to a website, or web page, that were bounces. A bounce rate of 10% means that one in ten of your website visitors only visited one page during their session. It's the same for individual pages. If your "about" page has a bounce rate of 50%, this means 50% of the sessions that included a visit to this page were single page visits.

The **exit rate** for a page shows the percentage of visits to the page that ended with users exiting the site from there. The diagram below shows how bounces and exits differ.

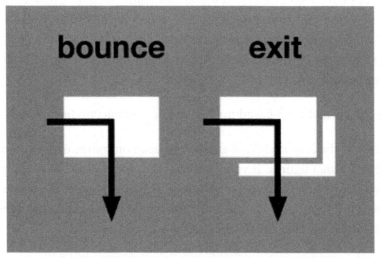

3-2. The difference between bounces and exits (credit: Danny Hope)

These two metrics are similar, but it's important to understand the difference between them. The bounce rate for a page is largely affected by the number of people who enter the website on that page. Often exit rate is a more useful metric to use for this reason.

It's worth mentioning that a high bounce or exit rate isn't always a bad thing. Users may land on a page, get the information they were looking for, and then leave happy. An example of this could be a user landing on the contact page of your website, finding your phone number and calling you. In this case, the user has achieved their objective quickly and efficiently.

We'll cover how best to use bounce and exit rates in your analysis later on. For now, though, just make sure you know the difference between the two.

Conversions and Goals

As described in the previous chapter, a **goal** is a notable action taken by a user on your website, or an action that's taken off-site, but fed into your analytics tool. An example of this could be a phone call, if you have call tracking software running on your website.

A goal could be as simple as viewing a particular page, or completing a particular form. Goals are often referred to as "conversions", but they're actually just one type of conversion. In Google Analytics, conversions also refer to purchases on ecommerce websites.

People often talk about a website's **conversion rate**. In Google Analytics, this is the percentage of visits that include a conversion—a user either triggering a goal or completing an ecommerce transaction. In other tools it may also refer to the percentage of unique users who have completed a conversion.

If the website in question is an ecommerce site, the term conversion will normally just refer to purchases. If the website isn't an ecommerce site, the conversion rate can either be a combined rate for all goals, or the conversion rate of the most important or primary goal.

As there's no consistent definition of what activity the conversion rate refers to, it's always good to check what someone means when they use the term.

A conversion is simply moving someone from one state to another. For example, moving someone who hasn't made a purchase to someone who has. Or even moving someone who doesn't like your brand to someone who does. Each desired conversion should be measurable in one way or another, and a goal or series of goals can be used to do this in analytics.

Segments and Filters

Analytics tools will generally provide options for segmenting or filtering your data. **Segmentation** describes grouping users with similar characteristics and viewing the data for those groups, often in comparison with other groups. An example would be segmenting your users by the device they used to visit your website—that is, by mobile, tablet or desktop. **Filtering** has a similar purpose, but it removes data from a certain group, or groups, leaving you with only the data from the group(s) that you want to collect.

In Google Analytics, filters and segments are separate options, but are often confused with each other.

Filters are applied at the view level of an account, and filter out information from ever being recorded in your reports. For example, if you filter out visits from your IP address for a view, that data simply won't be collected for that view. Filters are useful for excluding data that may otherwise skew your reports in ways you don't want.

Segments are applied at report level, and temporarily filter out information from all reports. For example, you might want to create a segment for mobile users from France. Once this segment is applied, all of your reports will only include data for French mobile users. The segment will stop being applied either when you manually remove it, or when you close Google Analytics and return. Segments can be really useful for analyzing the behavior of different user groups. We'll cover segmenting data in more detail later in this chapter.

A Guide to the Google Analytics Interface

As UXers, we've normally got strong opinions on design, and I've heard a lot of opinions on the user interface of Google Analytics!

Personally, I quite like the UI of Google Analytics, but I know plenty of people who think it's terrible and that it prevents them from doing more with their analytics. This section will help you find your way around the Google Analytics interface and help you get comfortable using it. Refer back to this section when you find yourself getting confused by the layout of your reports, or if you just want a refresher on how best to navigate the Analytics interface.

Navigating the Google Analytics Home Page

When you first log in to Google Analytics, you'll be presented with a page that shows you all of the accounts, properties and views you have access to. This page is the gateway to your reports, and it's fairly easy to navigate.

	Sessions	Avg. Session Duration
Brighton Digital Festival		
Luke Hay		
http://lukehay.co.uk (UA-23652227-1)		
Filtered view	327	00:01:48
lukehay.co.uk	406	00:01:39
lukehay.co.uk (all)	406	00:01:33
Test view	413	00:01:38
MB Skills & Coaching		
UX Brighton		
UX Camp Brighton		

3-3. The Google Analytics home page

Once you've clicked on a view, you'll be taken into the main Google Analytics reporting interface.

Navigating the Main Google Analytics Interface

There are around 80 different standard reports in Google Analytics, so enabling users to navigate between these is not an easy task. Google Analytics splits all the reports into four main categories:

- *Audience*: reports about your users, such as their demographics and where, geographically, they come from
- *Acquisition*: reports about how users arrived on your website, such as whether they came from organic search or via a referral link on another website
- *Behavior*: reports on what your users did on your website, such as what pages they viewed and how long they stayed
- *Conversions*: information about goal completions and ecommerce purchases.

The screenshot below shows this navigation, as well as other top-level navigation items:

3-4. Navigation in Google Analytics

Each numbered section in this image is described below.

1. Accounts, settings and diagnostics

The top of every page in Google Analytics displays the currently active account information, and provides controls that let you change settings, get help, and respond to diagnostic messages.

Click the downward arrow to access both your personal Google account, as well as your Google Analytics account. Use the account search box to quickly find Analytics accounts, properties, or views.

Click Settings (vertical ellipsis or cog) to change user settings or get help with Google Analytics.

Click Notifications (bell icon) to see any messages generated by Google Analytics' automated diagnostics.

2. Navigation links

Appearing throughout Google Analytics, the navigation links provide access to the four main product areas:

Home presents you with a list of all your Accounts and Properties, and gives you a quick overview of their performance.

Reporting gives you access to Google Analytics reports and dashboards.

Customization lets you create and view custom reports.

Admin is where you manage Google Analytics (create new properties, change user permissions, add integrations and so on).

3. Report navigation

In this left-had column of the page, use the search box to quickly locate a specific report. Click a report category to see the reports in that category.

Dashboards let you see your most important reports at a glance.

Use **Shortcuts** for faster access to the reports you use most often.

Intelligence Events monitor your website's traffic to detect significant statistical variations, and Analytics generates alerts when those variations occur.

Real-Time reports show the data for your website based on its current usage.

4. Segments

A **segment** is a subset of your Analytics data. Adding one or more segments to a report can help you compare and contrast your data in meaningful ways. This is where you can edit and set up segments to apply to your reports. Segments are good for creating personas, an area we'll cover in Chapter 5.

Navigating Google Analytics Graphs

Graphs play a big part in the Google Analytics interface. They're less useful than the raw data contained in tables, because they generally contain less detail. But they're still good for getting an at-a-glance idea of trends, and also for comparing different dimensions over time.

Click the **Reporting** menu option, and if you scroll down a little way you'll see a graph like this:

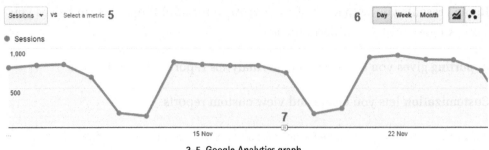

3-5. Google Analytics graph

5. Change graph metrics

You can change the primary metrics for the graph, and also add secondary metrics in. Adding secondary metrics will add a line to the graph. For example, you may want to compare *conversion rate* and *time on site* in a graph to see whether the conversion rate goes up as time on site increases.

6. Change graph display

Data points between lines can be shown on a daily, weekly or monthly basis. By default, most graphs use daily data points, but these can be hard to read if you're trying to analyze trends over time.

Changing to weekly or monthly will give a smoother impression, showing positive or negative trends rather than less useful daily spikes and troughs.

7. Annotations

As mentioned earlier, annotations are key to understanding what has happened previously to impact your metrics. Annotations can be both added and read from here.

Navigating Within Google Analytics Reports

Every report in Google Analytics has its own navigation. This enables you to filter data and to change how it's presented.

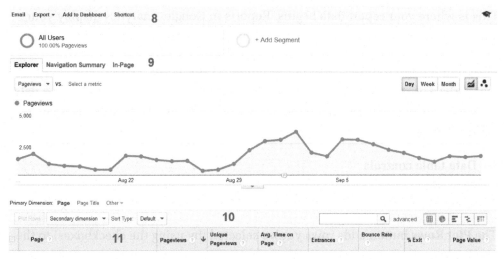

3-6. Navigation within Google Analytics reports

8. Report headers

A report header appears at the top of every report in Google Analytics. The header includes the report title and controls that act on the report as a whole.

The **Customize** link enables you to tailor a standard report to fit your specific needs.

The **Email** option lets you share a report with people, even if they don't have a Google Analytics account.

You can **Export** your report data for use in other applications, such as Excel.

Use the **Add to Dashboard** link enables you to embed the current report in a dashboard.

Shortcut creates a link to the current configuration of this report. You can access all your shortcuts in the report navigation panel.

The date selector (top right—not pictured) lets you change the date range of the report. You can compare two dates, or two ranges of dates by clicking the icon.

9. Report data

This is where your report data begins. Reports in Google Analytics display your data in one or more tabs, giving you multiple views of that data in a single place.

Most (but not all) standard reports contain an **Explorer** tab. Typically, this has two parts: a graph view of your data for the selected time frame on top, and a data table below. Some reports will show additional tabs, such as an **Overview** tab, or a **Map Overlay** tab.

10. Data table controls

This section of icons directly below the graph includes the following items.

The **Plot Rows** button adds rows you've selected (by using the checkboxes) to the graph view.

The **Secondary dimension** menu adds another dimension to the report as a new second column.

The **Sort Type** menu changes the order of the rows in the data table. Your choices are:

- **Default**: basic alphanumeric sort. Change the order by clicking the column header
- **Absolute change**: sorts date range comparison data by amount of change.
- **Weighted**: sorts percentage data in order of importance instead of numerical order.

The **Search** field displays only rows matching your search term. Click **advanced** to filter the data table in more complex ways.

The table display buttons change the way the data table is displayed. Your choices include:

- **Data**: the data in a tabular view. This is the default table view
- **Percentage**: a pie chart, showing the contribution to the total for the selected metric
- **Performance**: a horizontal bar chart, showing relative performance for a selected metric

- **Comparison**: a bar chart plotting the performance of the selected metrics relative to the site average
- **Term cloud**: a visual representation of the performance of keywords (not available for all reports)
- **Pivot**: rearranges the information in the table for certain reports by pivoting your data on a second dimension.

11. Tabular report data

The lower portion of the **Explorer** tab displays report data in tabular form. This is the area that you'll rely on most when analyzing data. Normally, the first column will contain your dimensions, while subsequent columns contain your metrics.

As you can see, there are lots of navigation options in the Google analytics UI. This can be overwhelming, but if you use this section as a reference, you should be able to find your way around without any major problems.

Analyzing Your Data

Now that you've got a good idea of what data is included in Google Analytics, and how to access it, let's have a look at some ways to analyze that data.

Analysis Over Time

It's important to look out for trends in your data. Viewing figures in isolation gives no context and means it's impossible to see the full picture.

As mentioned previously, you need to be aware of the seasonal factors that impact your website. Are you seeing an increase in traffic during the holiday season? How are conversion rates affected by the summer? Understanding seasonality will give you some of the context you need to understand why your metrics may be increasing or decreasing.

3-7. Comparing data over time

Comparing data from different time periods is particularly useful for giving context to the data. Google Analytics gives you the following date comparison options:

- **Previous period**. Selecting this will compare the current selected date range (normally 30 days by default) to the same time period prior to that. This ensures that you're comparing the same amount of data (e.g. 30 days worth of data).
- **Previous year**. Comparing to the previous year will pick exactly the same dates as you have selected from one year ago. Using this will help minimize the seasonal impact on the data.
- **Custom**. This option allows you to compare data from any dates you like. It's generally a good idea to still compare the same amount of data here. That is, if you have five days selected for your report, you'll often want to compare it to another five days' worth of past data.

When comparing data from the past, you'll normally want to ensure that you're comparing like for like. If, for example, you've selected five working days and you select **Previous period**, this will compare your data to the previous five days. This will be comparing the same amount of data, in terms of days, but may not be a fair comparison, as the **Previous period** data will include data from the weekend.

Comparing data over different dates can be really powerful, but be careful to compare equivalent data so as not to skew your results.

Analyzing Different Groups

As UXers, we're more aware than anybody that different people use websites in different ways. By default, your analytics package will generally include the data from all your visitors in your reports. This means you'll be lumping all your different types of user together. To get real insight into how users are really engaging with your website or app, you'll want to segment your data so that you can analyze your different user groups.

We'll cover how to use segments that match your user groups in Chapter 5. For top-level analysis, though, you can use basic system segments for comparison. In Google Analytics, the segmentation options are as follows:

- **System**. These are the default segment options that are available in all Google Analytics accounts.
- **Custom**. This is where you'll find the bespoke segments you've created.

To apply segments to your data, you'll need to click on the segments bar and then choose an option (or options) from the list:

3-8. Segments in Google Analytics

Once selected, your segment(s) will apply to all reports you go on to view. For top-level analysis, you may want to start by comparing the behavior of users on different device types, or users that come from different "sources" (for example, comparing users who arrived at your website via search with those who came via referral links on other websites).

Analyzing Data from Different Tools

We covered some of the different types of quantitative tools in Chapter 1. This book primarily focuses on website/app analytics tools, but these can be used alongside other tools for better insight.

You may also want to compare data from different website analytics tools to evaluate how accurate they are.

It's important to be aware that different data sources may be available, and to get the most out of your analysis you'll want to evaluate all available data.

Analyzing Data Outside of Your Analytics Packages

Reporting interfaces in analytics tools generally work well for most tasks, but there are times when you may want to do more with your data. In these cases, you may want to export that data to another tool.

Exporting Data As a CSV File

The most common way to analyze large amounts of data outside of your analytics tool is to export it as a CSV file, and then open it in Excel or another spreadsheet software package.

Once your data's in Excel, you'll be able to interrogate it to get the most from it. Common ways to analyze the data in Excel include:

- grouping pages together
- using pivot tables to manipulate data
- applying conditional formatting to highlight key metrics
- creating custom graphs

There are many uses for exporting your data as a CSV file. If you find yourself getting frustrated by the limitations of reports in your analytics tool, try exporting the data and interrogating it in Excel. (The article "Exporting your Google Analytics data"[1] provides some useful advice for exporting your data.)

[1.] http://www.stateofdigital.com/exporting-google-analytics-data/

Creating Reports in Google Sheets

There's a Google Analytics add-on[2] that allows you to create custom reports within Sheets. The add-on works by linking your existing Analytics account, using Google's Analytics API and Regular Expressions, to provide the data you want for your reports.

Getting the data directly into Sheets in a format that meets your requirements can be a real time saver. The add-on allows you to import any data from your Analytics account. You can then filter and segment this data, and also pull data from different time periods.

Once you've got everything set up, you'll be able to automate reports that show you the data you need.

Google Analytics Data Studio

Google has recently launched a new data visualization tool called Data Studio. Google Data Studio[3] provides a way for you to turn the data from your analytics tool into fully customizable visual reports.

Data Studio connects directly to different key data sources, so you can use data from different tools in the same report. This means you can spend more time analyzing the data and less time trying to pull it all together.

Adobe Analytics users can get access to a tool called Analysis Workspace[4], which offers similar functionality.

Analyzing for UX

Ensuring that your data is accurate before analyzing it is crucial. If your data is wrong, it's likely that any recommendations you make based on it will be wrong too.

---

[2] https://chrome.google.com/webstore/detail/google-analytics/fefimfimnhjjkomigakinmjileehfopp

[3] https://www.google.com./analytics/data-studio/

[4] https://marketing.adobe.com/resources/help/en_US/analytics/analysis-workspace/

Once you're confident your data is correct, and that all the information you need is being collected, you can begin to analyze it. You don't need a degree in statistics to do this—just a good understanding of the information you have available, and a clear idea of what you're looking for.

So far, this book has covered the best ways to analyze data. We've looked at how to get set up, the terminology involved, and how the Google Analytics user interface works.

The remainder of this book will focus on how analytics data can be used to help us achieve our UX goals.

Chapter

4

Finding Problems with Analytics

> The goal is to turn data into information, and information into insight.
> — *Carly Fiorina, Former CEO of HP*

Now that you're all set up and know how to analyze data, we can look into how to use analytics to find UX problems. I've worked on a wide range of websites across multiple industries, and my projects consistently begin with analytics. I firmly believe that an analytics-first approach is the best way to start any UX project where there is data available.

I follow a three-step process when I begin my analytics analysis:

- **Getting a feel for the website based on the analytics.** This involves identifying how many users visit the site daily, and which pages are the most popular, in terms of number of page views.

- **Breaking down the users.** I find out more about the users of the website by looking at their device, country and demographics.
- **Identifying potential problem areas.** Finally, I focus on identifying poorly performing pages and sections of the website.

The initial "eyeballing" approach gives me a top-level overview of the users of a website and how they're interacting with the site. I then move on to identifying areas where I can focus my UX work.

Before you can identify underperforming areas of a website or app, you'll first need to define what "underperforming" means. It's important that you have a clear idea of the objectives of the website that you're analyzing so you can evaluate it based on these. On a blog, for example, you may want to focus on page views, or the time users are spending on pages. For an ecommerce site, your primary focus will most likely be on transactions and revenue.

The following techniques will help you identify areas that are aren't contributing adequately to your objectives. You can then focus your efforts on improving them using other UX methods.

Individual Pages

A good starting point for identifying problem areas is to focus on individual pages. To begin with, common sense can be used as a starting point to identify key pages of the website. For example, in order to buy a product on an ecommerce website, users need to visit the checkout pages, so these are likely to be a focus.

You should also keep your objectives in mind when thinking about which pages are likely to be the most important. In addition to the pages you consider to be the most important, you'll also want to focus on the pages that have been visited the most. You'll need to consider quality as well as quantity here. If your list of top pages includes blog post pages with high volumes of low-quality traffic, they're less likely to be a focus of your UX work. Judge each page on its merits, rather than assuming high traffic equals high importance.

Looking at the Pages report in your analytics package will show page-level metrics for every page on your website. If I'm looking at Google Analytics data, I'll increase the number of results shown in the Pages report to the top 50 or 100 pages and focus on those to begin with.

Bounce and Exit Rates

In the previous chapter, we covered bounce and exit rates. These metrics tell us very little when applied to a whole website. However, when analyzed on a page-by-page basis, they can be very helpful in identifying potential issues.

A page with a high bounce rate may indicate that the content on the page wasn't what the user was expecting when they arrived there. But it could also mean that the user has found the information they were looking for and left the website having achieved their goal. An example of this could be the contact page of a site, or information such as opening hours for a shop.

A high exit rate may show that this page is causing the user to drop out partway through their intended journey. On the other hand, if the page with the high exit rate is the final page in the journey, then the exit rate is not a problem at all.

This is where you have to look at each page in context. Evaluate each high bounce or exit rate page individually, and decide whether the high rate is expected or whether it may point to an issue that needs addressing.

To quickly identify pages with high bounce or exit rates, I use the "comparison" option to compare the bounce rate and exit rate to the website average. This is a graph that shows whether pages are significantly above or below average for the selected metric. Be careful here, though. Just because a page has a better than average bounce rate may not mean it's performing well. The site average is a benchmark that may be getting dragged down by lots of poorly performing pages. Use the site average as a guide, but also make sure you're comparing the performance of a page to other well-visited pages, and to pages that perform a similar function.

4-1. Google Analytics comparison graph example

Doing this makes it easy to spot pages that have a particularly high bounce or exit rate compared with the site average.

If I notice a page with a high bounce or exit rate, I make note of it, in case something on that particular page is driving visitors away. The following screenshot shows that the "portfolio" page has a higher than average exit rate. This warrants some further investigation, as this page is not a natural exit point from the website.

4-2. Example of exit rates compared with the average

As well as looking at bounce and exit rates for the most visited pages, you may want to use **Weighted Sort**. According to Google Analytics, "Weighted Sort sorts percentage data in order of importance instead of numerical order." Using the Weighted Sort option in Google Analytics makes the bounce rate metric even more valuable.

Secondary dimension ▾	Sort Type:	Weighted ▾			

Page ?		Pageviews ?	Unique Pageviews ?	Avg. Time on Page ?	Entrances ?	Bounce Rate ? ↓
		4,660 % of Total: 95.73% (4,868)	3,185 % of Total: 93.87% (3,393)	00:01:32 Avg for View: 00:01:32 (0.07%)	2,517 % of Total: 92.43% (2,723)	46.68% Avg for View: 50.72% (-7.95%)
1. /blog/	⊕	434 (9.31%)	385 (12.09%)	00:01:48	299 (11.88%)	81.27%
2. /ux-services/	⊕	172 (3.69%)	152 (4.77%)	00:01:28	66 (2.62%)	93.94%
3. /2015/06/measuring-marginal-gains/	⊕	79 (1.70%)	67 (2.10%)	00:03:05	58 (2.30%)	82.76%

4-3. Weighted Sort in Google Analytics

To give an example, a page may have a 100% bounce rate, but if it only had one visit in the last month, then only one person left the page (and a bigger issue may be that no one is visiting the page!). If the page has an 80% bounce rate, but is one of the most visited pages on your website, this will be of more concern and should lead to further investigation.

Time on Page

The **average time on page** metric is, as you would expect, the average amount of time users spend viewing a web page.

As covered in Chapter 2, though, time-based metrics are often inaccurate, so be careful when analyzing this figure. If your web pages don't have many views (say, fewer than 50), the average time can easily be skewed. You certainly shouldn't make any decisions based on time-based metrics alone, but they can still provide an indication of an issue.

Context is key when considering a high or low time on page. Ideally, you want users to be able to move through a checkout page quickly. So if they're spending a lot of time on that page, it might be because the page is overly complicated and they're overwhelmed with information. On the other hand, if a blog post has a high average time on page, it's generally a good sign, since it implies that users are actually reading the whole post.

Time-based metrics are best used in conjunction with other metrics to get a rounded idea of the performance of a web page.

Page Value

Page Value is a way to give a single web page a direct monetary value. For ecommerce sites, it pulls in the values from transaction revenue, and for all other types of websites (both of which need to be set up manually in Google Analytics for a page value to be calculated), it pulls in the goal value.

 Differing Nomenclature

Different analytics packages have different ways of referring a monetary value to a page. In Adobe Analytics, this metric is called "Participation". In Google Analytics, it's called "Page Value".

A high page value will often be a sign of an important page, which indicates that it's a good page to focus on during usability tests.

$$\frac{\text{Transaction Revenue} + \text{Total Goal Value}}{\text{Unique Page Views for the page}} = \text{Page Value}$$

4-4. Page value formula

The formula above may look complicated, but when broken down, it's actually quite simple, and incredibly useful.

 Be Careful With Ecommerce Sites

If ecommerce sites have goals with values assigned to them, Google Analytics will add the page value of goals and purchase conversions. This can be avoided by setting up different views for goal page value and ecommerce page value.

Ecommerce Revenue

If somebody makes a purchase during their visit to your website, the amount they spent will be recorded as **ecommerce revenue** within Google Analytics. You can use this metric to calculate additional metrics like per-visit value. As long as you have ecommerce tracking set up correctly, ecommerce revenue will be calculated automatically by Google Analytics. Non-ecommerce websites need to use "goal value" to assign a monetary value to a visit—which we'll look at next.

Goal Value

Even if you don't offer ecommerce functionality on your website, users will still perform tasks that will be worth money to you. Let's take an example of a travel agent who offers luxury holidays but doesn't take bookings online. Instead, they'll ask users to contact them to arrange their holiday—normally by telephone or email. In this case, a user completing a contact form will not always lead to a transaction, but it will (hopefully) be the starting point for many transactions. Over time, our travel agent will get a good idea of approximately how many people who contact them actually go on to make a booking.

If the average cost of booking a holiday through our luxury travel agent is $5000, and roughly one in ten people who get in contact end up booking, we can say that each person who gets in contact is worth $500.

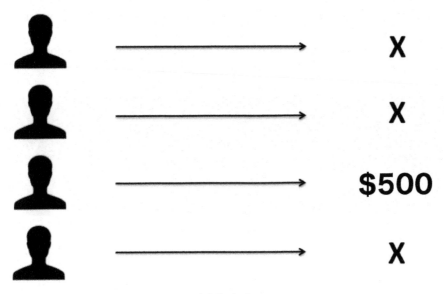

4-5. Goal value

This $500 gives us our **goal value**. This is a useful metric for working out the value generated by a non-ecommerce website, and is also a key component of working out page value.

Assigning a value to a goal by working back from ultimate conversion value is the ideal, but not always possible. Sometimes, for example, a lead-generation site offers so many products or services that working out an average goal value is impossible.

However, there are two alternative methods for assigning goal values that are also very useful. If you can get data to show that one type of goal is of more value than another, you can still assign *relative* goal values. For example, if you know that phone calls convert at 20%, but form enquiries convert at 10%, you might want to assign goal values of $20 and $10 respectively. This means that, when looking at the page value scores of pages, you can still build a picture of how valuable individual pages are across all weighted goals.

The last option, if you can't give individual goals weighted values, is to give them all an arbitrary value—for example, $100. (Larger numbers are better to help avoid Google giving values less than $0.1). This will at least provide some page value score to help you establish which pages are important to *any* conversion.

Now that you have a good understanding of ecommerce revenue and goal value, let's have another look at the page value formula.

$$\frac{Transaction\ Revenue\ +\ Total\ Goal\ Value}{Unique\ Page\ Views\ for\ the\ page} = Page\ Value$$

4-6. Page value formula

Ecommerce revenue and goal value are added together to give a total value, and this is divided by the number of unique page views for a page involved in the conversion. This is best explained by looking at where pages appear in user journeys. The diagram below shows four simple user journeys on an ecommerce website.

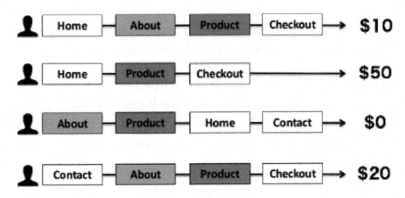

4-7. Page values by user journey

As shown in the image above, three of the four journeys that occurred ended in transactions, while one did not. Looking at these journeys, we can quite easily calculate page values based on the amount of revenue taken, divided by the number of times each individual page has been viewed. In the example below, the product page appeared in all four user journeys, so we can work out its value by adding together the revenue for all four journeys ($10 + $50 + $0 + $20) and then dividing that by the number of unique page views (four).

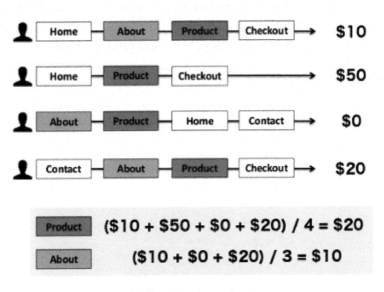

4-8. Page values by user journey

Fortunately, you won't need to do any manual calculations here, as Google Analytics will do that for you. Getting these figures from other analytics packages is normally possible, but can require manual calculations.

It's important to know how page value is calculated, though, as you'll need to understand what this metric represents and what it means from a UX perspective. A simple way to think about it is that page value represents how often a page features in a customer journey that ends in a conversion—with the size of their transaction also taken into account.

Pages with a high page value are key points in the conversion process. Cart and checkout pages, for example, will naturally have high page values.

Page value in itself can be a good metric to use to identify the most "important" pages on a website. This can give you a good starting point for where to focus your UX efforts. However, page value is particularly useful for identifying under-performing pages.

High-value pages that show a high exit rate are a good area to focus on for improvement. These are pages where users are dropping out at a key part of their journey to conversion. In the example below, taken from an ecommerce site I worked on, I've highlighted three categories with a similar page value. There's clearly a far higher exit rate for the "Wooden Toys" product page.

Page		Pageviews ↓	Unique Pageviews	% Exit	Page Value
1. /					
2.					
3. /wooden-toys				7.26%	
4. /toys-games				2.68%	
5. /wooden-toys/				21.75%	£4.04 (55.51%)
6. /personalised-toys				7.31%	£4.24 (61.22%)
7.					
8. /home-and-outdoors					
9. /toys-games/				8.41%	£4.30 (62.13%)
10.					

4-9. Page values in Google Analytics

The image shows that this is a high value page that's "leaking" users, and should be the focus of future UX work. This could mean a heuristic assessment of this page, or focusing a user testing task on the page. Remember, the analytics tells us the What; we need to use other UX methods to find out the Why.

Leakage

As covered in the previous section, high value pages with high numbers of exits can be thought of as "leaking" users, and leaking value. To help to identify which pages are the most responsible for leaking value, you can use a formula that was created by Fresh Egg, an agency I currently work with in the UK.

4-10. Leakage formula

The formula is quite simple, and can be quickly calculated for all pages of your website by exporting your data into Excel and performing a simple calculation. The result of this will be a leakage value for each page. The pages with the highest leakage are the ones you'll want to focus your UX efforts on.

 Exclude Pages With Naturally High Leakage

Some pages—such as confirmation pages—will naturally have high leakage, and therefore might not be a UX focus. Use common sense here to pull out any pages you feel don't need your focus.

404 Error Pages

The final area you'll want to investigate in order to uncover problem pages is to look for any 404 errors. Technically, these pages are broken rather than underperforming, but your analytics package will give you an easy way to identify them.

The best way to find 404 pages is to switch the dimension from page, or URL, to "page title". As long as your 404 page has an easily identifiable title, you should be able to find it in your report.

You can then view all the "pages" with this title to see which URLs are commonly showing errors. You'll be able to use the navigation reports (which we'll cover later on in this chapter) to find out how users are finding these 404 pages. You can then fix broken links and help users find their way around your website.

Underperforming Content

Looking at individual pages is a great way to find out where there are problems on your website. However, it may not be practical to look at every single page on a website, for two reasons:

1. Large websites can contain hundreds and thousands of pages, making analyzing them all very time consuming.

2. If pages serve a similar purpose and use the same template (such as product pages), looking at them in isolation will not give you an accurate picture of how that page type is performing.

For this reason, it can be highly beneficial to group similar or related pages together. One way to achieve this is by exporting page-level data and adding or averaging metrics in Excel or another spreadsheet package. But this can be time consuming, and can get messy if you're dealing with large amounts of data. Fortunately there's a way to combine the data for related page in Google Analytics using the Content Grouping feature.

 Grouping Templates Together

> If you export page-level data, you still need to find a way to group templates together. If the URLs or page titles have template identifiers in them, you can do group analysis using filters within Google Analytics without needing to export. Use the search box above the Pages report to apply a temporary filter to the report before exporting.

Content Grouping

The purpose of **Content Grouping** is to group certain web pages together in a way that will replicate how you see your website. Rather than looking at individual pages, you'll be able to see the data for certain *types* of pages.

A simple example would be to group all of your blog posts separately from the rest of your site. Or, if you have an ecommerce site, you might want to group your pages into product categories.

If you sell clothing online, you might want to group pages into men's/women's/children's clothing, or by type of clothing, with trousers/sweaters/T-shirts/accessories as your grouping. This gives you a great way to show the differences in user behavior between each type of content. You can now see at a glance whether dresses have a higher bounce rate than trousers!

You can also get an average page value for each content group, showing you which types of content are the most valuable to you.

Setting up and reading the reports is fairly simple, but the key step—as with most data analysis—is ensuring that they're set up to give you data that's relevant to you. For this, you really need to start thinking about what you want to learn about your content *before* setting anything up. If you're planning to set up content grouping, your setup should be unique for each website, as all sites are different.

Let's say you run an ecommerce website selling a range of clothes for men, women and children. The first step would be to think of possible page groupings. In this case, some ideas for groupings might include:

- **product type**: e.g. hats or socks
- **product category**: e.g. men, women or children
- **product price**: e.g. expensive, cheap etc.
- **page type**: e.g. category, product, checkout

Next, you should think about what you would do with that data. The product type grouping could be useful for marketing, and for telling you more about your users, but it's unlikely to identify many fixable problems. The product category may help to show age- or gender-specific issues, while the price category may tell you how price-sensitive your users are. In terms of fixing problems, though, the page type category will likely be the most useful. This can help show at which stage of the buying process users are experiencing difficulties. It would be very difficult to asses the performance of your product pages without grouping them, particularly if you stock hundreds of different products.

One of my clients runs an ecommerce site selling electrical goods. I set up different types of content grouping for them, one of which split their pages into categories based around the different types of page on the site. This helped me to analyze the grouped product pages against the category pages. This came in useful for identifying the areas that had the most potential for improvement.

Primary Dimension: Page   Page Title   Content Grouping: Page Type (Content Group) ▾   Other ▾

	Page Type (Content Group) ?	Page Views ? ↓	Unique Views 3 (Page Type) ?	Avg. Time on Page ?
		1,111,656	519,449	00:00:59
		% of Total: 100.00% (1,111,656)	% of Total: 100.00% (519,449)	Avg for View: 00:00:59 (0.00%)
☐	1. Subcategory page	558,872 (50.27%)	219,481 (42.25%)	00:00:57
☐	2. Product page	245,474 (22.08%)	134,503 (25.89%)	00:01:21
☐	3. Category page	95,924 (8.63%)	55,670 (10.72%)	00:00:36
☐	4. Checkout and Order details	46,346 (4.17%)	8,611 (1.66%)	00:01:02
☐	5. Blog page	33,991 (3.06%)	30,716 (5.91%)	00:01:31

4-11. Content grouping in Google Analytics

The following screenshot shows the Content Grouping report. This can be found in Google Analytics by visiting **Behavior > Site Content > All Pages** and then using the Content Group dropdown above the table.

Primary Dimension: Page   Page Title   Content Grouping: Page Type (Content Group) ▾   Other ▾

Page type detail (Content Group)
Product Category (Content Group)
✓ Page Type (Content Group)

	Page Type (Content Group) ?	Page Views	Views 3 (Page	Avg. Time on Page ?
		1,111,656	519,449	00:00:59
		% of Total: 100.00% (1,111,656)	% of Total: 100.00% (519,449)	Avg for View: 00:00:59 (0.00%)
☐	1. Subcategory page	558,872 (50.27%)	219,481 (42.25%)	00:00:57
☐	2. Product page	245,474 (22.08%)	134,503 (25.89%)	00:01:21
☐	3. Category page	95,924 (8.63%)	55,670 (10.72%)	00:00:36
☐	4. Checkout and Order details	46,346 (4.17%)	8,611 (1.66%)	00:01:02
☐	5. Blog page	33,991 (3.06%)	30,716 (5.91%)	00:01:31
☐	6. Search Pages	33,365 (3.00%)	10,524 (2.03%)	00:00:55

4-12. Content Grouping location in Google Analytics

Using content grouping here allowed me to see that the blog section of the website had a high exit rate and a low page value. This isn't uncommon for blog pages, but it showed there was an opportunity to improve the cross-linking between the blog and other, ecommerce-related sections of the website. Doing this led to a decrease in the exit rate and an increase in page value for blog pages.

Another client I set up content grouping for was a recruitment agent with an active jobs board. Here I grouped the content by types of jobs to see whether, for example, accountancy jobs had a higher bounce rate than IT jobs. This gave me a better idea of how different types of users engaged with the content, and allowed me to make recommendations on the type of content to produce for each of those different user groups.

Content groups should be analyzed in a similar way to individual pages. Look for any groups with high bounce or exit rates, those with a low time on page, and groups with a particularly high or low page value. Once those groups have been identified, your first step should be to look for any clear UX or technical issues on these pages, using your experience and judgement. After this, you should test the page (or pages) with real users, to find out *why* they're experiencing these issues, and gather clues for how to improve them.

There are lots of different ways to group your content, and you can have multiple groupings for single websites. Content Grouping is completely customizable, so it enables you to set up groups that match your own individual requirements and objectives. Spend some time thinking about what you want to get from your reports before setting up your groupings, and then go ahead and begin grouping your pages to make your analysis more efficient.

User Journeys

Looking at pages, or groups of pages, in isolation will only ever tell you part of the story. As UX practitioners, we know the importance of looking at the entire user journey. Understanding how users navigate their way through your website is vital to understanding the issues they may face. Most analytics tools will include reports showing how users navigate between your pages, and these reports should form a key part of your analysis.

Identifying Drop-off Points

Knowing how users move through a website can add context to single-page stats. For example, analyzing previous pages on a user journey may help to indicate why the exit rate of a particular page is so high. An example of this could be if pricing is different on category pages and product pages. This could cause users to exit *product* pages, when, in fact, the pricing issue might actually be on the previous page.

In addition, identifying the common user journeys through a website can be very beneficial when it comes to composing tasks for a usability test. Your usability test tasks can be created to mirror those common user journeys, ensuring that the behavior of users during tests is in line with that of existing site users.

Google Analytics attempts to show user journeys with the User Flow and Behavior Flow reports. In User Flow and Behavior Flow reports, pages are visualized as green boxes with grey lines showing the user journeys between them. Each box also shows the percentage of **drop-offs**, in red, where users are leaving the site. They can help demonstrate popular user journeys, and where users are exiting the site, which can be another indication of problem areas.

These can be hard to read, and often suffer from grouping multiple pages together, meaning that Google Analytics will often only show the top few most popular pages individually, but will then combine several pages and label them as ">100 pages", which is of no help at all! Unlike content grouping, where you purposely group similar pages to make analysis easier, you have no control over the "grouping" that appears in the flow reports. Here, the pages that are grouped together may have nothing in common and be grouped because there's not enough space to display them all on the flow report.

The screenshot below shows how only a few individual pages are displayed for each step of the journey before pages are grouped, making analysis difficult due to this limited information.

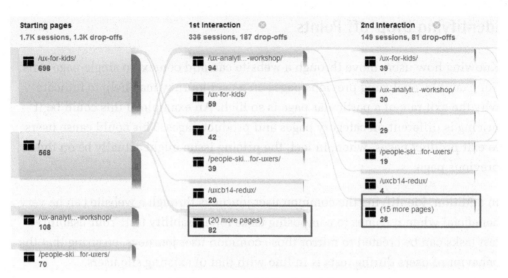

4-13. User flow report in Google Analytics

Despite the issues caused by page grouping, spending time analyzing these reports can help to identify problem areas based on drop-off rates or unexpected user journeys. (For example, did a user go in a very different direction than expected?) Once we identify the problem areas, we can create usability testing tasks to see how users are thinking as they go through the journey, and learn why they're having trouble.

The example below comes from a travel site that I worked on, which featured a prominent search box on the home page.

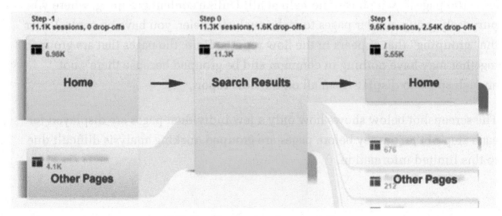

4-14. User flow for a travel agent website

In this annotated and simplified picture, it's quite easy to spot a potential issue. Visitors were using the search box to find a holiday destination, but then returning back to the home page from the search results page (aka "pogo sticking"). This demonstrated that the search results shown were unsatisfactory in some way. This could have been due to a number of reasons. Perhaps the search was regularly returning no results, too many results, or too few results. It could be that the problem was not with the search results themselves, but another factor—such as the prices for the holidays shown on the search results being too high.

 Pogo sticking

> **Pogo sticking** is where a user navigates to a page deeper in a site's hierarchy, only to immediately navigate back to the page they just came from. This typically happens multiple times in a row, and is likely to cause a large amount of frustration for your users!

Because the data suggested the initial search was unsatisfactory, I did some usability testing on the search box. This revealed that the search results were too broad, and users were overwhelmed by the number of results. Based on the outcomes of the user testing, I suggested introducing a faceted search system on the results page, allowing users to filter results on a range of criteria without having to start their search again from the home page. The new search system allowed users to filter their results by the facilities offered—such as whether the hotels in the results had swimming pools, gyms and other amenities. This meant users were able to find results that were useful to them. The design solution led to a large reduction in the number of users returning to the home page after their initial search, and saw more users reaching the next step of their journey.

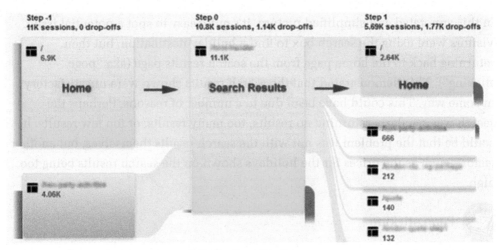

4-15. User flow, after changes

The screenshot above shows the analytics for the month after faceted search was introduced. It shows a reduction in pogo sticking between the home page and search results. There was clearly still room for improvement, but it was encouraging to see positive results from the change.

Navigating Between Individual Pages

While the Behavior and User Flow reports can be used to show complete journeys through a website, it's also beneficial to focus on individual steps within that journey. The best way to do this with Google Analytics is to use the Navigation report.

To view the navigation to and from an individual page, you'll need to follow these steps:

1. Navigate to the Pages report (**Behavior > Site Content > All Pages**).
2. Click on the page in the report that you'd like to analyze.
3. On the resulting page, click on the Navigation Summary tab.

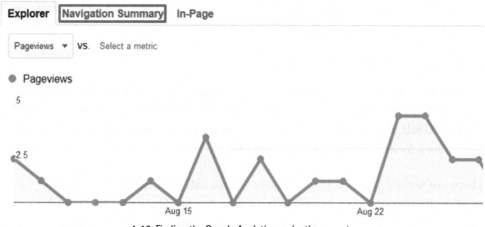

4-16. Finding the Google Analytics navigation report

On the Navigation reports, you'll be shown a list of the previous and next pages.

Current Selection: /training/ Show rows: 10

Exits Jan 1, 2015 - Sep 7, 2016: 43.15%

Next Pages Jan 1, 2015 - Sep 7, 2016: 56.85%

Next Page Path		Pageviews	% Pageviews
/ux-services/		23	18.70%
/contact/		22	17.89%
/		17	13.82%
/my-work-portfolio/		14	11.38%
/2014/12/google-analytics-training-special-offer/		12	9.76%

4-17. The Google Analytics Navigation report

In the example above, taken from my own website, we can see that users are going from the home page to my training page, and then moving to the UX services and contact pages. These seem like reasonable pathways to take, though ideally I'd like to reduce the exit rate from the training page and also reduce the number of people returning to my home page from here.

Goal Funnels

As covered earlier on in this book, **goals** are notable actions taken by users on a website. Goals are the main indicator of the success of a website, and therefore should be a focal point of your UX analysis.

There are several types of goal, but one way to categorize them is to decide whether they're one-step or multi-step goals. A user signing up to a newsletter is likely to be a one-step goal. The user will have completed the goal as soon as they enter an email address into a form and then click "subscribe". This type of goal is completed on one page, and as one "step". Other types of goals require users to complete different steps across different pages. An example of this would be a checkout on an ecommerce site. A checkout may follow several steps before the user completes their purchase:

- accessing the cart page and clicking to the checkout
- entering address details
- choosing a delivery option
- entering payment details
- reviewing and confirming an order

These steps give a lot of potential drop-off points for the user, and, as a result, give us an opportunity to analyze this journey.

In Google Analytics, funnels can be set up for all multi-step goals. An example of a funnel report can be seen in the following screenshot.

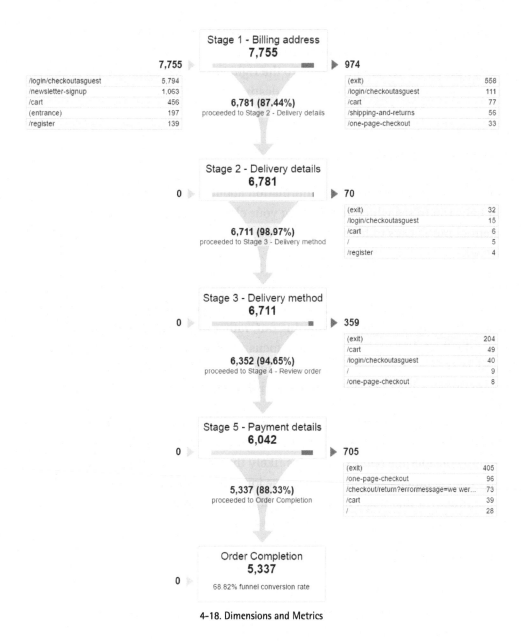

		Stage 1 - Billing address **7,755**		
7,755 ▶			▶ 974	
/login/checkoutasguest	5,794		(exit)	558
/newsletter-signup	1,063		/login/checkoutasguest	111
/cart	456	**6,781 (87.44%)**	/cart	77
(entrance)	197	proceeded to Stage 2 - Delivery details	/shipping-and-returns	56
/register	139		/one-page-checkout	33

	Stage 2 - Delivery details **6,781**		
0 ▶		▶ 70	
		(exit)	32
		/login/checkoutasguest	15
	6,711 (98.97%)	/cart	6
	proceeded to Stage 3 - Delivery method	/	5
		/register	4

	Stage 3 - Delivery method **6,711**		
0 ▶		▶ 359	
		(exit)	204
		/cart	49
	6,352 (94.65%)	/login/checkoutasguest	40
	proceeded to Stage 4 - Review order	/	9
		/one-page-checkout	8

	Stage 5 - Payment details **6,042**		
0 ▶		▶ 705	
		(exit)	405
		/one-page-checkout	96
	5,337 (88.33%)	/checkout/return?errormessage=we wer...	73
	proceeded to Order Completion	/cart	39
		/	28

	Order Completion **5,337**
0 ▶	
	68.82% funnel conversion rate

4-18. Dimensions and Metrics

This report shows the funnel for a typical checkout. The boxes in the middle represent pages in the checkout process. These are identified by the title at the top of each box (e.g. "Add to Cart"). The number below the title is the number of views each of these pages has received during the reporting period. The green and red bars below the page view number represent the number of users who have exited at this stage (red) and those that have proceeded to the next step in the funnel (green). The arrows between the boxes show the figures relating to the green and red bars. Here we can clearly see the number, and percentage, of users who've proceeded to the next step. To the right are shown the pages users entered the funnel from, and to the left are the destination pages for users who've dropped out of the funnel.

Analyzing Funnels

Funnels give you a lot of useful information about crucial user journeys. They can help you to see which pages along your checkout process are causing potential purchasers to leave your site and possibly buy from your competitor instead!

One starting point for analyzing a funnel is to look at the steps with the highest percentage of drop-outs. But you should also consider volume here. By "volume" I mean the *number* of people dropping out, rather than the percentage. For example, it might be more valuable to focus on an area where there's a large number of users dropping out early in the journey, rather than to focus on an area where there's a high percentage of users dropping out.

In the case of the previous example, the highest percentage drop-off would be the first step (users moving from the cart to the billing details page). However, we need to consider the context here. It's likely that more users will drop out at this stage than at other stages of the purchase journey, as they've made less commitment at this stage. It's common for users to add products to their cart but then have a change of heart before progressing.

There are several reasons for this, including:

- It's easy to add an item to the cart: users just need to click a button. After doing this, though, they need to enter information and put in some work themselves. The prospect of this may be enough to put some users off.
- There may be more information on the cart page (such as delivery cost details) that may put users off progressing.
- At the cart stage, users can be distracted by elements such as discount code boxes or invitations to "carry on shopping". Users may be taken away from the checkout journey, and not all of them will return.

Users may also have added products as a wish list, or for a product comparison, with no immediate intention to make a purchase.

When analyzing the funnel, you'll need to keep in mind that the drop-out rates for each step will naturally differ due to their context. With funnels, my main focus is on the later steps in the process. By the final step, users have invested time and effort to get there, and have no real reason not to go on and complete their purchase. Drop-outs at this stage could represent your best opportunity for making improvements.

One way to evaluate this would be to apply a weighted value to each step completed towards the final conversion. This could be a dollar value, which increases by a certain amount towards 100% at each step from start to end. This means that, if a conversion is worth $100, step one could be worth $5, step two $20, step three $60 and so on. This can be set arbitrarily, but it allows you to have a subjective way of assessing where the most important drop-outs occur: number-of-dropouts x value.

Going back to our example funnel, my main areas of focus would be the "proceed to payment page" step and the final "proceed to sales confirmation" step.

As covered previously, drop-outs towards the end of the funnel are a concern. At this stage, our user would have entered all their information, and now just needs to press the "confirm" button to complete their purchase. Failure to do so suggests there's a problem with the final page in our funnel.

This could be because:

- there's a lack of reassurance that the user is making the right choice in buying from your website
- there's a usability issue with the page, making completing the purchase more difficult than just clicking a single button
- users have been surprised by new information, such as being shown delivery details for the first time, which may put them off

There are lots of other potential reasons, but remember: it's not the job of the analytics software to tell us what those are. That's your job as a UX practitioner.

The other area of concern on the example funnel is perhaps more obvious. Nearly a third of users are failing to complete their billing details. These users are committed enough to have begun the checkout process, but have been put off at this crucial stage. There are, of course, possibly reasons for this that are out of your control—such as users having problems finding their credit card, or realizing they can't afford your product. But you need to make this first step of the process as easy as possible, to maximize the number of users moving to the next step.

Again, it's not the job of your analytics package (or the job of this book!) to tell you what the problem might be. The analytics will tell you *what* is happening where otherwise you might just be guessing. This will help you focus your efforts on the areas likely to lead to the maximum increase in conversions.

It's always worth remembering that it's extremely unlikely you'll be able to get everyone to move all the way through the funnel. You need to keep your expectations realistic here, but still, there's nearly always going to be some room for improvement and optimization of your funnel.

The other big benefit of funnels, as with most analytics reports, is that they can be used to measure the impact of any changes you make. We'll cover this side of things in more detail in Chapter 6.

Interactions with On-page Elements

As well as looking at the performance of individual pages and different user journeys, it's important that you also look at what users are doing *on* those pages. Most analytics packages will only focus on page view data by default—meaning that on-page engagement data is missed out on. Here are some examples of on-page engagement that aren't generally measured by analytics packages by default:

- playing of a video
- scrolling up and down a page
- interacting with form fields
- using filters on search results or product lists
- downloading items
- clicking on outbound links

▨ interacting with live chat functionality

As you can see, there's a lot a user can do on your website without even leaving the page they land on. This behavior should be monitored, as it will tell you a lot about your users' behavior. There are several different tools and techniques that can be used to track on-page behavior.

Event Tracking

With Google Analytics, and some other analytics packages, code can be added to elements of a web page to track clicks on that element. This is known as **Event Tracking** in Google Analytics, and it gives you a lot of additional insight if implemented correctly.

With just a small amount of additional code, you can start collecting data on a whole host of additional activities that happen on your website which won't be tracked with the standard Google Analytics code. Your event tracking will be completely custom to you, so you can set it up in a way that's easy for you to understand. Event tracking passes the following data onto Google Analytics:

▨ **Category**: helps to categorize different types of events. Examples of categories include "videos" and "downloads".
▨ **Action**: describes the type of action taken by the user. An example of this would be play, or pause, for a video.
▨ **Label**: gives a way of differentiating between different items in a category. If the category is "videos", the labels would be for individual videos such as "product demo video".
▨ **Value**: the value field is optional, and works in a similar way to goal value. If you think someone watching your video is worth $5 to you, then include a value of 5 in your event tracking.

Once you've set up event tracking, you'll be able to see the reports in the **Behavior > Events section**. Spend some time analyzing this data to get a better idea how users are interacting with on-page content on your website. You can create custom reports and advanced segments to gain even more insight. For example, you could see whether people are more or less likely to convert after watching your product video.

For more on this, the Koozai website's blog has an excellent guide to setting up and monitoring event tracking[1].

Click Mapping

A lot of the techniques described in this book use Google Analytics, or similar analytics tools, to help you achieve your UX goals.

However, there are other tools that can give you valuable insight into user behavior on your website. Click-mapping tools, such as Crazy Egg and Hotjar, will show you where users are clicking on your pages. Unlike web analytics packages, these tools often require you to specify the pages whose activity you want to record. This means they're best set up when you have a clear idea (from your web analytics data) which pages are key to the performance of your website. They can be used as another way of identifying potential problems on these pages.

These click-mapping tools produce heat maps to show where the activity is happening on your web pages.

We can work out some of that information using a web analytics tool, but it takes a long time to analyze the data, and we wouldn't have the "at a glance" nature of a click map.

However, click maps can be hard to analyze. They also sometimes show little or no insightful data, so be careful not to spend hours staring at a map expecting it to answer all your questions! Click maps only show one aspect of user behavior—where the user clicks. This doesn't tell you *why* they clicked, or what they were thinking.

Click maps are often better utilized to help to confirm or deny existing suspicions about user behavior.

---

[1] https://www.koozai.com/blog/analytics/the-complete-google-analytics-event-tracking-guide-plus-10-amazing-examples/

Scroll Mapping

Tools like Crazy Egg and Hotjar include both click and scroll mapping functionality. **Scroll mapping** shows you how users are scrolling on pages of your website—something which web analytics packages (like Google Analytics) don't cover. Scroll maps display a visual representation of the amount of time visitors spend viewing each section of the page. As with click maps, scroll maps will only record activity on specified pages. This means you'll need to analyze your website analytics carefully to identify your key pages, and then set them up to have their scrolling behavior recorded.

Session Recordings

Tools like Hot Jar also offer session recording. These tools can help to identify usability issues by enabling you to view recordings of real visitors on your site. The videos show where they click, tap, move their cursor, type and navigate across pages. But they don't record any audio, or show the faces of your users! This means you still don't know what your user is thinking or feeling. Still, these videos can help to identify issues, such as users clicking on the wrong place on a web page, or scrolling past your main call-to-action button.

Discovering "Hidden" Content

Analytics will show us the content users are viewing, and can also show us how they're interacting with that content. This analysis will tell you what users are doing, but not necessarily what they're trying to do. To find out user intent, you'll normally have to rely on user research. There is an exception, though. Looking at the search terms they use on your website will often give a clear indication of what a user is trying to achieve. I think of this type of content as being "hidden". This is content that users are looking for but find hard to reach.

Many analytics tools will report on the activity of users interacting with the search box on a website. Reporting on search usage will normally require manual setup, but this is quite straightforward, and it will give you access to some very useful information.

Search vs No Search

The first detail you'll want to look at in your internal search reports is to find out how many of your users are engaging with your search box. In Google Analytics, this is found in the Search Usage report, which is located at **Behavior > Site Search > Usage**.

This report not only tells you what percentage of your users are engaging with your search box, but it also allows you to compare the behavior of searchers and non-searchers. This can help you to identify how useful search is in delivering visits that convert. The figure below shows a search usage report for an ecommerce website.

Site Search Status	Sessions ↓	Transactions	Revenue	E-commerce Conversion Rate
	347,585 % of Total: 100.00% (347,585)	5,563 % of Total: 100.00% (5,563)	£448,835.12 % of Total: 100.00% (£448,835.12)	1.60% Avg for View: 1.60% (0.00%)
1. Visits Without Site Search	**337,044** (96.97%)	4,774 (85.82%)	£387,289.40 (86.29%)	1.42%
2. Visits With Site Search	**10,541** (3.03%)	789 (14.18%)	£61,545.72 (13.71%)	7.49%

4-19. Search usage in Google Analytics

It's clear from the table that visits utilizing search are far more likely to convert than those that don't. This may mean that, if you encourage more users to search your website, your conversions will increase. Be careful not to make any assumptions here, though. It's likely that users who are typing into the search box are arriving on your website with a clear idea of what they're looking for, and, as a result, they're naturally more likely to make a purchase than users who come to your website to browse.

This is the very common "correlation vs causation" quandary, which can most accurately be solved by running an A/B test, where the search box is given additional prominence in the variation. We'll cover A/B testing in more detail in Chapter 6.

There are other metrics in the table that are useful for analysis. Looking at average time on site and number of pages per session will help you get a better idea of how the behavior of searchers and non-searches differs. But always keep in mind that the "non-searchers" will include all single-page visits—and it's highly likely that they'll view fewer pages and spend a shorter amount of time on the site.

Search Terms

As well as giving an overview of the behavior of searchers and non-searchers, your analytics package will be able to record the search terms they use. In Google Analytics, this can be found in **Behavior > Site Search > Search Terms**. The screenshot below shows the Search Terms report for a website that sells traditional toys.

Search Term ?	Total Unique Searches ? ↓	Results Pageviews / Search ?	% Search Exits ?
	52,876 % of Total: 100.00% (52,876)	**1.32** Avg for View: 1.32 (0.00%)	**14.25%** Avg for View: 14.25% (0.00%)
1. wooden toys	**482** (0.91%)	1.40	5.60%
2. stocking fillers	**278** (0.53%)	1.16	45.68%
3. dolls house	**176** (0.33%)	2.14	32.39%
4. personalised notebooks	**158** (0.30%)	1.30	36.71%
5. bath toys	**140** (0.26%)	3.95	36.43%

4-20. Search terms in Google Analytics

These search terms tell us exactly what our users were looking for. Search terms fall into one of two categories:

- terms relating to products/content on the site
- terms relating to products/content not on the site

The above may seem obvious, but it's an important distinction to make. The category these search terms fall into will shape your next course of action.

If the content or product that a user is searching for is already on your site, you should consider whether it's currently easy enough to find. If a lot of users are searching for the same thing, it may be that this is harder to find than it needs to be. If you think this is the case, you should run user testing, asking users to find the elusive item and see where they're experiencing problems. If you find users are having genuine problems finding it, and not just resorting to search as the easy option, you'll want to make it more prominent and easier to access.

When it comes to analyzing search terms, you also want to consider alternate names for something, such as "sneakers" or "trainers".

If the content or product a user is searching for is not already on your website, this may give you an opportunity. If I notice, for example, that a lot users are searching my site for information about a particular analytics feature, I would give serious consideration to writing a blog post about it. The same is true for products on ecommerce websites. If you sell wine glasses, but you notice a large number of users are searching for whiskey glasses, you'll want to look at the possibility of stocking whiskey glasses too. In this instance, the search terms used show a demand. It's up to you to decide if you're able to meet that demand.

Pages Where Search Is Used

The final area of the internal search reports you'll want to analyze is the Pages report. In Google Analytics, this can be found in **Behavior > Site Search > Pages**.

This report is useful for pinpointing possible "dead ends" on your website. Analyzing this report shouldn't take long, but have a quick look and see if there are any surprises there. Are there pages high up on this list that you wouldn't expect users to be searching from? If so, take another look at those pages and see how you can improve the navigation from them.

The Pages report also allows you to drill down into the data and view the search terms used on each page. These may give you a clue as to why users are searching from this point, and could provide you with an obvious destination for your additional navigation. For example, if lots of people were searching for "Google Analytics training" on my blog post pages, I would consider adding a link to the training section of my site at the bottom of every blog post.

Internal search data can be extremely valuable for understanding user intent. It can help you to identify problem areas on your website in a way that no other data will. But remember: be careful not to read too much into these reports on their own. Keep using your other analysis methods to prove or disprove your theories.

Device and Browser-specific Issues

It's important to break down your analytics to see the performance of different audiences. Your website may look quite different on different devices and browsers, and your analytics data can help you uncover issues that may otherwise require huge amounts of testing.

Browsers

We've all experienced the problem of websites not working as they should in certain browsers. (Internet Explorer, aka IE, is often the culprit!) Cross-browser testing can be a boring and time-consuming process. Fortunately, most analytics packages will allow you to break down your visitors by the browser they used when visiting your site.

In Google Analytics, the browsers report can be found in **Audience > Technology > Browser & OS**. This report will show you metrics relating to all the different types of browsers used to visit your website. The following screenshot shows this report for an ecommerce site.

Browser ?	Sessions ? ↓	Transactions ?	Revenue ?	E-commerce Conversion Rate ?
Desktop only (new)	**45,844** % of Total: 61.95% (74,005)	**1,041** % of Total: 68.40% (1,522)	**£63,374.05** % of Total: 76.19% (£83,176.46)	**2.27%** Avg for View: 2.06% (10.41%)
1. Internet Explorer	**18,489** (40.33%)	367 (35.25%)	£23,923.35 (37.75%)	1.98%
2. Chrome	**16,605** (36.22%)	395 (37.94%)	£23,754.24 (37.48%)	2.38%
3. Firefox	**4,421** (9.64%)	94 (9.03%)	£5,391.71 (8.51%)	2.13%
4. Edge	**2,810** (6.13%)	91 (8.74%)	£4,877.61 (7.70%)	3.24%
5. Safari	**2,679** (5.84%)	89 (8.55%)	£5,083.74 (8.02%)	3.32%

4-21. Browser report in Google Analytics

As this is an ecommerce website, my focus is on the conversion rate. In this instance, we can see that the conversion rate is lower in Internet Explorer than in the other major browsers. This suggest there may be an issue we should look into. Clicking on "Internet Explorer" from here will drill down and show data relating to different versions of IE. The screenshot below shows the breakdown of visits by different versions of Internet Explorer.

Browser Version ?	Sessions ? ↓	Transactions ?	Revenue ?	E-commerce Conversion Rate ?
Desktop only (new)	**18,489** % of Total: 24.98% (74,005)	**367** % of Total: 24.11% (1,522)	**£23,923.35** % of Total: 28.76% (£83,176.46)	**1.98%** Avg for View: 2.06% (-3.48%)
1. 11.0	**12,195** (65.96%)	324 (88.28%)	£20,746.96 (86.72%)	2.66%
2. 8.0	**2,804** (15.17%)	5 (1.36%)	£235.94 (0.99%)	0.18%
3. 9.0	**2,223** (12.02%)	20 (5.45%)	£1,093.95 (4.57%)	0.90%
4. 10.0	**1,039** (5.62%)	17 (4.63%)	£1,774.52 (7.42%)	1.64%

4-22. Internet Explorer data

In the above example, we can see that the conversion rate from older versions of Internet Explorer is very low. This may just be a coincidence, but it certainly merits further investigation. In this particular case, viewing the website in Internet Explorer 8 showed that the drop-down navigation was broken, making it very difficult to navigate the site.

It's not practical, or even possible, to view your website on every version of every browser. The browser reports in your analytics package will help you find any potential issues—assisting you in finding that needle in the haystack. Using tools like BrowserStack[2] can help you get a quick overview of how your website renders in different browsers. There's no substitute for manual checking, though, so that you see your website in the same way your users do.

Devices

Most analytics packages will also allow you to break down your visitors by the type of device they used to visit your website. You'll normally be able to view the device category (desktop, tablet or mobile) and also the device type (such us iPhone or iPad).

Looking at the Device Category will give you an indication of how users convert across desktop, tablet and mobile. When viewing the Devices overview report in Google Analytics (**Audience > Mobile > Overview**), I like to use the pie chart option to quickly and clearly see the breakdown of visits by device category.

I then switch back to the table view to see the full data. My focus here is primarily on comparing the bounce rates, pages per session and conversion rates across the different categories.

It's important to keep in mind that the metrics for mobile devices are quite likely to be worse than those from desktop. It's likely to be unrealistic to think that mobile and desktop conversion rates will be the same. For ecommerce websites globally, stats show that desktop conversion rates are around four times higher than those for mobile visitors[3].

In some cases, this will be down to the context people use their devices in, while in others it could be due to poor mobile design. Low conversion rates on mobile

---

[2.] https://www.browserstack.com/

[3.] http://www.smartinsights.com/ecommerce/ecommerce-analytics/ecommerce-conversion-rates/

may still show a good opportunity for design improvement, so they're still well worth investigating.

When comparing device category conversion rates, it's often best to look at trends over time to see the impact that changes have made.

As well as the Device Category report, it's worth spending time analyzing the data for different types of device. Doing this will show popular device types, which you should use to test your changes. It will also show you conversion rates on different device types.

Mobile Device Info ?	Sessions ? ↓	% New Sessions ?	Ecommerce Conversion Rate ?
	49,118 % of Total: 30.41% (161,522)	**61.35%** Avg for View: 61.20% (0.26%)	**2.62%** Avg for View: 7.88% (-66.74%)
1. Apple iPhone	**35,346** (71.96%)	60.20%	3.02%
2. Samsung SM-G900F Galaxy S5	**1,533** (3.12%)	61.25%	2.54%
3. Samsung SM-G920F Galaxy S6	**762** (1.55%)	64.17%	2.89%
4. Samsung GT-I9505 Galaxy S IV	**689** (1.40%)	59.36%	1.12%
5. Sony D5803 Xperia Z3 Compact	**518** (1.05%)	64.86%	2.90%

4-23. Data for different device types

As we can see from the screenshot above, there's a potential issue with the Samsung Galaxy S4, where the conversion rate is far lower than the average. The next step here would be to have a good look at your website using this type of device and see if you can spot any issue that may be preventing your users from converting. If you don't have access to that particular device, the next best option is to use emulator tools, or services like BrowserStack.

Finding Problems with Analytics

There are several techniques you can use to help uncover potential problem areas by using your analytics. Begin by getting a "feel" for the available data, and then move on to segmenting your visitors to gain a better understanding of how different types of users are engaging with your website.

Once you have a good understanding of how people are using your site, you can begin to identify potential problems in the following areas:

- individual pages
- groups of pages
- user journeys
- goal funnels
- in-page interactions
- internal search
- devices and browsers

Exploring these areas should give you a great idea of where to focus your UX efforts to make improvements.

In the next chapter, we'll look at how you can use your analytics data to help inform your user research.

Chapter

5

Analytics for User Research

> The price of light is less than the cost of darkness.
> —*Arthur C. Nielsen, Founder of ACNielsen*

Knowing who your users are is crucial to any UX process. This is why user research plays such a vital role. **User research** consists of a whole range of different tools and techniques, but what underpins them all is gathering useful data.

Research is not about asking people what they like or what they hate, but establishing facts about your users. This ties in with analytics, where data is objective, providing facts rather than opinions.

This chapter will cover how your analytics data can support and inform your user research. The data you get from your analytics tool is no substitute for in-depth user research, but taking an analytics-first approach to research will help you build strong foundations.

Where Analytics Sits in the Research Process

There's no one, fixed model for the user research process. Different people will approach user research in different ways, and the process may change depending on the project.

The following diagram shows some of the different forms of user research you might use as part of your process.

5-1. Where analytics fits in with some common user research methods (credit: Tim Minor)

Continuing the theme of an "analytics-first" approach, the diagram shows how analytics can be the starting point for other types of user research.

Your data can be used at the start of your process to get a broad idea of the types of users visiting your website. It can also be used to help you create detailed personas, and to analyze the behavior of different user types. Use your analytics data to support your other research methods to get the most out of the process.

Knowing Your Users

To understand why your users behave the way they do, you first need to get to know them. You may make assumptions about who those users are, but you should be constantly challenging those assumptions, or at least be backing them up with facts.

There's a lot of data available in your analytics package that will help build up your knowledge of who's visiting your website. The more you know about your users, the more informed your design decisions can be.

This data can form a useful starting point for many different types of research. One area where this data is particularly helpful is in recruiting people for usability tests. In usability testing, the better the participant matches the target persona, the better the test.

Usability testing should show how "real" users interact with your website, and where they may be experiencing issues. Knowing who your users are will improve the results of your usability testing, and will give you a better chance of uncovering the issues your "real" users are encountering.

The following section looks at the data in your analytics tool that will help build up your understanding of who your users are.

How Do Users Find Your Website?

Analyzing how users are finding your website can help you understand more about them, and about the context of their visit.

Different analytics tools will classify "traffic sources" or "channels" in different ways. The following are some typical sources for your traffic:

- **Organic search**. This typically identifies a user who has clicked an "unpaid" link from the search results.

- **Paid search**. Paid search users, sometimes known as "Pay Per Click" or "PPC", will have arrived on your website via a paid advert on a search engine.
- **Referral**. Users from referral links will have followed a link from another website.
- **Social**. Social media is often shown as a separate channel from other referral links.
- **Direct**. This category includes users who type your domain into the address bar of their browser. It can also include users where the analytics package was unable to identify their traffic source.
- **Email**. Links in emails will need to be tagged, since by default, analytics tools are unable to identify users clicking links that don't appear on web pages.

This analysis can give you a better idea about your users' intentions. If you're running a paid search campaign, for example, you'll be able to see the keywords that were used to find your website (as long as you've linked up the Google Analytics and Adwords accounts, and enabled auto-tagging). If users are finding you based on "brand" search terms, you know they're aware of your company and are searching for you specifically.

Analyzing the behavioral metrics for users, broken down by channel, can help content and marketing teams make decisions about the amount of effort, resources, and budget to dedicate to specific channels. From a UX perspective, it can be useful for identifying problem areas (see Chapter 4), but it also helps to give insight into the mindset of your users. Knowing where your users are coming from can help you to identify whether they're already familiar with your website, and can start to give you clues about the likely purpose of their visit.

Where Do Your Users Come From?

To begin with, it's a good idea to start by finding out where—geographically speaking—your users come from. This is a very broad level of analysis that will help you focus your research. Looking at the location of your users will show you the role international visitors play in the success of your website. Geodata will also give you insight into the behavior of users on a national and regional level.

Most analytics tools will give you location data for your users. In Google Analytics, this can be found in **Audience > Geo > Location**. This report will tell you where your users are coming from, and will also allow you to compare behavior metrics (and different dimensions) for users from different countries, regions or cities.

Country	Acquisition			Behavior		
	Sessions ↓	% New Sessions	New Users	Bounce Rate	Pages / Session	Avg. Session Duration
	94,573 % of Total: 100.00% (94,573)	81.50% Avg for View: 81.44% (0.08%)	77,081 % of Total: 100.08% (77,022)	50.92% Avg for View: 50.92% (0.00%)	4.00 Avg for View: 4.00 (0.00%)	00:02:10 Avg for View: 00:02:10 (0.00%)
1. United States	33,444 (35.36%)	68.59%	22,938 (29.76%)	30.41%	6.66	00:03:39
2. India	4,986 (5.27%)	90.75%	4,525 (5.87%)	64.38%	2.45	00:01:26
3. Thailand	3,944 (4.17%)	94.98%	3,746 (4.86%)	72.39%	1.52	00:00:33
4. Turkey	3,879 (4.10%)	93.48%	3,626 (4.70%)	68.08%	1.55	00:00:30
5. Brazil	3,303 (3.49%)	93.88%	3,101 (4.02%)	69.00%	1.83	00:00:49

5-2. Location report in Google Analytics

Looking at the percentage of visitors from each country will help you understand the importance of international visitors to your website.

But you need to be careful with your analysis here. Just because no one visits your site from Canada, for example, doesn't necessarily mean that audience is not important to you. You could be accidentally blocking them! Your marketing efforts may not be reaching where they should, or there may be a whole host of other reasons for the lack of visits. Once again, remember that your website analytics tell you *what*, but not *why*.

You may be assuming your website only attracts visitors from your own country, but this report may show that you should also consider the needs of international visitors. This could lead to practical considerations—such as the load speed of your website in other countries, international delivery rates for an ecommerce site, and possible cultural differences between other countries and your own.

Cultural differences based on the country of your visitors can be considerations for both your website's design and functionality. These differences can be hard to cater for, as cultural differences may be subtle, and often won't lead to clear ideas for design changes. Still, detailed research on the cultural needs of you users is definitely recommended.

On a more practical level, the way people use ecommerce websites varies dramatically depending on their country. According to data from Worldpay[1], only 12% of users in Germany make online purchases using cards.

This compares with 63% of UK users and 72% of users in the USA. If you notice that your ecommerce website is getting a lot of visits from Germany, you'll want to look at offering alternative payment methods. The most popular type of online payment in Germany in real-time bank transfer.

Looking beyond the number of visits, you'll be able to see behavioral metrics, such as time on site, bounce rate and conversion rate. Focusing on user behavior will enable you to pinpoint particular countries where there may be issues with your website, and thus opportunities to make improvements. If, for example, your ecommerce website is getting a lot of visits from a certain country, or countries, but the conversion rate is low, you may want to reassure those users that you deliver internationally.

There could be many reasons why your conversion rate is low in a particular country. You may not ship to that country, your site may be in the wrong language, the products may be cheaper in that country, or you may not offer the right payment methods (as in the example of Germany). This is where it's important not to jump to conclusions. Remember, the data only tells you *what* is happening. It's important that you set aside research time to find out *why*.

If you can see an opportunity to increase your conversion rate internationally, you might also want to consider personalizing your website in some way for those countries. This could be as simple as showing the flag of that country and being up front about the exact costs and delivery times for that location. This simple form of personalization will likely resonate with your international users, and will help you unlock potential additional revenue from international sales.

If your analytics shows you're getting a lot of visits from other countries, you're likely to be missing out if you don't factor in cultural differences!

[1.] https://alternativepayments.worldpay.com/territories/DE

Geo reports can locate users down to state and city level. This means you may also want to assess your visitors by state, region and city to get a clearer picture of who your visitors are and how they behave. The importance of this level of detail will depend on the purpose of your website. For political websites, for example, localized data can be very important to see how a candidate is performing in a key state or region.

What Language Do Your Users Speak?

Knowing what language your users speak can give you additional insight into the content you should serve up. Language and location are sometimes confused when looking at analytics, but the two dimensions have no direct connection. A user can be located in Paris but speak Spanish. Location is ascertained by the IP address of your user, while their language can be derived from the language settings of their browser.

You may notice you're getting a lot of visits from German-speaking users. If this is the case, you might want to look into creating a German version of your site if you don't already have one.

As with location, language can also give an indication of the culture of your users. The language used can also have a big impact on your design. Arabic text is displayed from right to left, and the Chinese alphabet contains thousands of characters. Both of these will potentially have a big impact on your page layouts.

For example, websites targeted at Chinese audiences are likely to contain a lot of links, rather than offering users search options. This is due to Chinese keyboards being more difficult to use than western keyboards, because of the large number of characters in the Chinese alphabet.

You may be surprised to learn about a larger than expected audience you had no idea existed. It's likely that users who don't share your language will be "silent", and, as a result, may be overlooked and unrepresented when it comes to your user research. By "silent", I mean these users are less likely to contact you or offer feedback than users who share your language.

Finding out the languages used by your visitors is, of course, just a starting point. I wouldn't recommend making any major changes based on this data alone. But it can play a very useful role in your user research process.

What Devices and Browsers Are They Using?

When you know which devices are being used to visit your site, you get a clearer picture of the context in which users are viewing your website. Analyzing browser usage can also help you better understand your users.

In user research, you should be careful not to rely on stereotypes or to make broad assumptions about your users. That said, knowing which browsers and devices they're using can help you get a broad sense of their demographics.

These kinds of studies may help you hypothesize why your users are behaving differently, but I certainly wouldn't use them on their own. Find out more about your users to test these hypotheses.

Device information is likely to tell you even more about your users. While you also need to be careful about assumptions, research shows, for example, that adults in higher-income households are more than three times as likely as those in lower-income households to own a tablet[2]. There are also differences in the demographics of users of different device brands. A study has shown that iPhone users are better qualified and more affluent than Android users[3].

As with the previous example, there's some value in these studies, but you need to be very careful how you apply it. Remember, the analytics data will tell you *what* is happening, but you'll need to do further research to find out *why*.

A common mistake analysts make with device reports is to assume that mobile users are "on the move" (such as commuting), while "desktops" are always used at home. A study by Google[4] showed over 60% of mobile usage is at home, while

---

[2] http://www.marketingcharts.com/online/the-demographics-of-us-smartphone-and-tablet-users-60669/

[3] http://www.forbes.com/sites/toddhixon/2014/04/10/what-kind-of-person-prefers-an-iphone/#6afb33213e5a

[4] https://www.thinkwithgoogle.com/research-studies/the-new-multi-screen-world-study.html

the "desktop" device category includes laptops, which people are likely to use while traveling.

You need to be careful how you use device and browser data. Don't make assumptions about your users based on the data alone, but instead let it help shape your research.

Knowing the breakdown of browser and device types can also help identify who to recruit for user testing. If you know that 75% of your users are visiting your site on a mobile device, you'll probably want to ensure the majority of your user testing takes place on mobile.

What are the Genders and Ages of Your Users?

Seeing how users from different demographic groups behave on a site can really help build up a picture of the different user types. In 2013, Google Analytics introduced demographic reports, which include information on users' age, gender and interests. These reports are a potential gold mine for user research. It's hard to tell exactly how accurate they really are, but the demographic data that Google Analytics reports is usually very similar to my own expectations for sites I know well. Google claims the reports 80–90% accurate, and a study by Humix[5] concludes that the demographic data held by Google appears to be quite accurate.

When I get a new analytics client, I often ask them about what they expect the breakdown of the age and gender of their users to be. I then compare this to the reports in Google Analytics—and they're often very similar. While I'd wouldn't recommend treating this data as if it's 100% accurate, based on my experience I'd say you can be fairly confident it gives a good representation of the age and gender of your users. If possible, I also recommend testing this yourself, by surveying a sample of site users and correlating the results against the same user segment in Google Analytics.

This information can be used to directly inform your personas, and to aid with your usability testing recruitment. You can also use this information to confirm, and fix, some concerns you may have about your audience.

[5.] http://www.humix.be/en/blog/web-analytics-en/how-accurate-are-google-analytics-demographics-reports/

I'm one of the organizers of UX Camp Brighton[6], an annual UX "unconference" that takes place in my home town of Brighton in the UK. Recently, along with my fellow organizers, I had concerns about the gender balance of our attendees. As with most tech events, we were generally getting more male than female attendees, and we were keen to redress this balance. Checking the demographics report for our website confirmed that we did in fact have a far larger percentage of male visitors. Armed with this knowledge, we partnered with Spring Forward[7], a series of events celebrating the role of women in digital culture. We both promoted each other's events, and the result was a measurable increase in the percentage of women viewing our website.

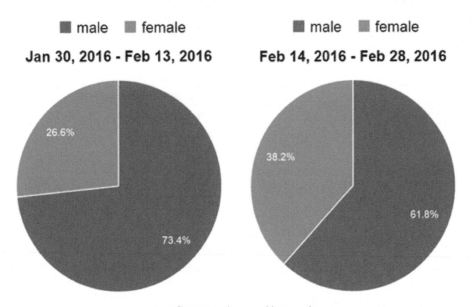

5-3. Changes to demographics over time

We don't collect gender data for ticket sales, so we can't say for sure whether it changed the audience for the event, but it was certainly a step in the right direction, and is something we'll look to do again next year.

As well as age and gender, the demographics reports in Google Analytics give data on the interests of your users. Personally, I find these reports less useful than the other demographic reports. I often see the same, very generic interest groups

---

[6.] https://www.uxcampbrighton.org/

[7.] http://wespringforward.com/

appearing. Some of the categories are very broad, such as "movie lovers" and "TV lovers", and probably apply to 90% of people in every community!

How Frequently Are Your Users Visiting?

Your analytics tool will be able to help you gauge the loyalty of your users. Users who keep returning to your site are likely to behave differently from first-time visitors. Grouping your users in this way can be helpful when you're creating user types or personas.

Below is a screenshot of a typical Frequency & Recency report from Google Analytics. This can be accessed by going to **Audience > Behavior > Frequency & Recency**

Count of Sessions	Sessions
1	8,732
2	1,956
3	893
4	500
5	335
6	231
7	181
8	139
9-14	491
15-25	325
26-50	245
51-100	100
101-200	94

5-4. Frequency and Recency report

We can see the majority of visitors only visited once during the selected time period of 30 days. At first glance, this suggests you only need to focus on that group. But if you add the users who visited more than once together, you'll see they make up nearly 40% of the total.

It can be helpful here to break these users down into groups that better meet your research requirements. You might want to group users as single visits, 2–10 visits, and 11+ visits. You can then label these groups as "one-off", "repeat visitors" and "regular visitors". This will give you a broad but useful overview of how often your users visit your site.

What Content Are They Interested In?

In the previous chapter, we covered how to identify problem pages or areas on your website. The Pages report can also be useful for finding out what type of content your users are interested in.

For example, if you're looking at data for a real estate website, you may be able to group users into buyers, sellers, renters and letters, depending on the pages they're viewing. This may not be an easy task, as users won't always look just at pages targeted to them. In the real estate example, it's likely people looking to sell their property will also look at properties already on sale to check prices. In this instance, you may need to choose pages further down the funnel to help group your users more accurately.

This type of information will be useful for various aspects of your research, including creating personas.

Using Data for Personas

Personas are used in the UX process to represent actual users of a website. They're generally created to aid the decision making for the design process, and can be a powerful tool to help keep the focus on users at all times. The wealth of data available to you in your analytics package can be used as a starting point for creating new personas, and also used to analyze how those personas are using your website.

Using Data for Persona Creation

Personas aren't real people, but they represent real people—the types of people likely to use your website. The best ones are not just "made up", but instead formed from in-depth knowledge of the website users and their likely behavior. As we've covered, your analytics data gives you information on demographics that can be useful for creating personas based on details of real users.

There are several methods for getting the information needed to create realistic personas for your site. Some information may be gained by talking to stakeholders who may have first-hand experience of their users. User research of some kind is also vital, though, and could include surveys and in-person interviews with real users. Your analytics should also play a big part in persona creation.

Using the data from your Audience reports will help get you started in the persona creation process. In fact, almost any metric in Google Analytics can be used to help shape personas. Time on site, for example, may give an indication of whether your users are pushed for time or are likely to be leisurely browsers, while a high bounce rate may signal impatience and/or efficiency.

The key to creating truly accurate and useful personas is to draw from a range of sources to get a complete picture. I'm not recommending that you only use Google Analytics, but it certainly provides a lot of unbiased data, which can only help with the process. Don't use analytics data in isolation. Use it alongside other research methods, rather than instead of them.

 Don't Use Analytics Data Blindly When Creating Personas

While analytics data can be useful for persona creation, it can be tempting to rely too heavily on this data, which could lead to inaccurate personas. For example, if you're creating two personas for a website and your data tells you there's a 50/50 split of male and female users, it makes sense to have one male and one female persona. If the same website has 50% of visits from the UK and 50% from the USA, though, what would that mean for your personas? Should you make the male persona from the UK or USA? There's no way of answering that with the data alone. This further underlines the need to do more user research to get a clearer picture of who your users really are.

Persona creation is a bit of an art form, and is not the subject of this book! I certainly wouldn't recommend only using data from your analytics tool to base your personas on. Instead, consider this data as a starting point for other research methods.

Creating Persona-based Segments

Once you've got a good idea who your users are, you can create segments to see how different groups of users are behaving on your site. A **segment** is a subset of your analytics data. For example, a segment might be made up of users from a particular country or city. Another segment might be mobile users, or users who visit a particular section of your website. Segments can be made up of a single dimension, or multiple dimensions, such as French-speaking women using tablets.

In Google Analytics, you can create custom segments by clicking the Segments bar at the top of your reports.

From here, you can select from a list of predefined "System Segments", or create your own segments to use. To create your own segments, click **New Segment** and then select your chosen dimensions.

From the New Segments menu, you can create your segment based on any of the data stored by Google Analytics. In the example below, I've set up a segment for women visiting my site from the UK.

Demographics

Segment your users by demographic information.

Age ⑦	☐ 18-24 ☐ 25-34 ☐ 35-44 ☐ 45-54 ☐ 55-64 ☐ 65+
Gender ⑦	☑ Female ☐ Male ☐ Unknown
Language ⑦	contains ▾
Affinity Category (reach) ⑦	contains ▾
In-Market Segment ⑦	contains ▾
Other Category ⑦	contains ▾
Location ⑦	Country ▾ contains ▾ United Kingdom ⊗

5-5. Setting up advanced segments

Under the Advanced options, you can select whether you want to base your segmented data on sessions or users, as well as creating segments based on users following specific pathways through your website.

As you can imagine, Google Analytics enables you to create very specific segments that can match your different user types or personas.

Using Persona-based Segments

Once you have your segments, you can apply them and view your navigational reports (either in the Site Content section or in the User Flow reports) to see how representatives of your personas are interacting with your site.

As well as looking at their paths through the site, you can begin to focus on the main exit pages for your persona groups, or to look at which user types are most likely to make a purchase. You may find one particular segment has a high exit rate at a particular stage of your checkout funnel, for example.

Because you can apply up to four segments at any one time, using persona-based segments will allow you to compare the behavior of your different user types. In the example below, we can see the differences in behavior of two different types of users—men and women.

Entrances		Exits	
Male users: 67.69%		Male users: 30.11%	
Female Users: 69.52%		Female Users: 26.95%	

Previous Pages		Next Pages	
Male users: 32.31%		Male users: 69.89%	
Female Users: 30.48%		Female Users: 73.05%	

Previous Page Path	Page Views	% Page Views	Next Page Path	Page Views	% Page Views
/checkout/cart/			/checkout/onepage/success/		
Male users	204	32.96%	Male users	217	12.81%
Female Users	193	28.64%	Female Users	239	10.49%
/			/contact-us		
Male users	55	8.89%	Male users	171	10.09%
Female Users	62	9.20%	Female Users	262	11.50%

5-6. Navigation by different genders

Whether you're running side-by-side comparisons, or doing a deep dive into the details of one particular user type, persona-based segments are a vital part of your UX analytics analysis.

This whole process can be cyclical, too. You can use Google Analytics data to inform your personas, and then use those personas to interrogate your data further.

Benchmarking Against Competitors

In my training sessions, people often ask me things like, "My bounce rate is 47%; is this good or bad?" My answer is always the classic UX response: "It depends".

I've touched on why a high bounce rate can be good or bad, and why it's important to analyze your bounce rate on a page (rather than a site) level. Another factor to consider is how it compares to similar types of websites. Different sizes of websites, websites targeting different countries, and websites in different industries will have varying metrics. To find this data, look at the options available for benchmarking your website against your competitors.

You can learn a lot by analyzing how your users behave on your site. But to gain additional context, you should also consider how your competitors' sites are performing.

Competitor research can form part of your user research process—and you're able to do some basic competitor research, for comparison purposes, using Google Analytics.

Benchmarking in Google Analytics

As I mentioned in the first chapter of this book, Google Analytics is the most popular website analytics tool on the market. It's used on millions of websites, and, as a result, Google has access to a *lot* of analytics data. Back in 2013, Google decided to make some of this data available within its benchmarking feature.

About the Benchmark Reports

Benchmark reports allow you to compare your website metrics with those of similar websites in your industry. These reports can be found in **Audience > Benchmarking**. There are three types of benchmarking reports indicating how your site is performing against competitors:

- **Channels**: lists the channels users have followed to arrive at your site.
- **Location**: shows the countries, or regions, from which users have arrived at your site.
- **Devices**: lists the devices used by site visitors.

Each report uses the same set of metrics:

- Sessions
- % New Sessions
- New Users
- Pages/Session
- Avg. Session Duration
- Bounce rate

Google Analytics offers three indicators of sites similar to your own for benchmarking purposes:

- **Industry Vertical**: for example, real estate > property management
- **Geographical region**: for example, United States > all regions
- **Traffic size**: for example, 500 to 999 daily sessions

Benchmark reports enable you to alter these indicators within each report. This means that you can change your site's vertical and compare its performance to alternative business types, locations and sizes.

For the industry vertical, there are over 16,000 options, so you should be able to find a vertical that's a good match for your site.

Using the Benchmark Reports

The first step in using the benchmarking reports is to check the indicators at the top of the report to ensure they're appropriate for your website.

5-7. Benchmarking report indicators

You'll need to select the most appropriate industry vertical for your site. With the geographical region, you'll want to either select the country the majority of your users come from, or you may want to select "All" if you have an international website. You shouldn't need to change the traffic size option, as Google Analytics works this out automatically based on your data.

Once you're confident you have accurate indicators, you can start to look at how your website is performing against your competitor benchmark. Be aware that this isn't necessarily going to include all of your direct competitors. This data will give you an indication of how you're performing against websites in your industry of a similar size.

The first of the reports shows how your website is performing against its competitors across different channels. This type of report is generally of more interest to marketers, who'll be interested in comparing the performance of traffic sources against the benchmark.

The second benchmarking report allows you to analyze data on how your website stacks up against its competitors in different countries. This is more useful to us, as it can provide extra context for the cultural differences I mentioned earlier in this chapter. It can help answer questions such as, "Is my bounce rate high in China due to an on-site issue, or is it due to bounce rates being higher in China in general?", or, "Is my website failing to reach a specific state, or is that state just not interested in my type of product?" Answering these types of question can ensure you're not trying to fix problems that don't exist.

The final benchmarking report in Google Analytics focuses on device usage. For me, this is often the most useful of the benchmarking reports. Here you can see how your website is performing on mobile and tablet devices against your competitors.

There's usually a big difference in the way mobile and desktop users interact with your site. But without context, it's hard to gauge whether your mobile site is performing better or worse than you'd expect. If my bounce rate on desktop is 40%, is a 50% bounce rate on mobile to be expected, or is it a cause for concern? Device benchmarking reports will go some way toward answering that question. You're able to see how the bounce rates of your competitors vary between device types. Keep in mind this is only one single indicator, and won't answer all your questions. It's also worth remembering that metrics like bounce rate and time on site are not the best indicators of the performance of your website. If your figures differ substantially from the benchmark, though, you may want to investigate further.

The ability to work out the breakdown of visits by device for your competitors is another really useful feature. One of my clients, who runs a global jobs board, believed they received fewer visits from mobile devices than their competitors. This was based on a hunch, but data from Google Analytics confirmed this was the case, and I was able to give him accurate figures on how their device breakdown compared to similar-sized jobs boards.

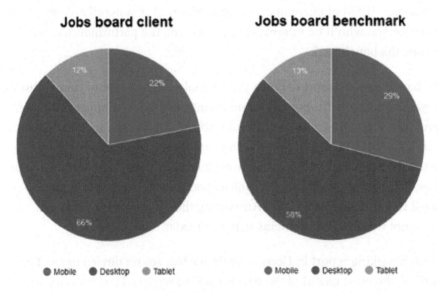

5-8. Benchmark comparison

This data is available in Google Analytics, but you'll need to work out the percentage breakdown yourself. The data shown in Google Analytics is the number of sessions; I just copied it into Excel to work out the percentages and create the pie charts.

The benchmarking reports in Google Analytics are great for giving additional context to your data. They're missing some key metrics, such as conversion rates, but the information that's available can be really useful for getting insight into how your website is performing.

Other Benchmarking Techniques

The benchmarking reports in Google Analytics are useful, but they're quite limited. I often use other sources to find competitor data for benchmarking purposes. As I touched on in the previous section, one key metric that's missing from the Google Analytics benchmarking reports is conversion rates. The conversion rate is arguably the most important metric for many websites, particularly ecommerce sites. Without context, it's difficult to know what a good or bad conversion rate is.

Desk research will help you to find industry statistics on conversion rates. Websites like smartinsights.com and monetate.com post quarterly statistics on conversion rates across different device types and different countries. This type of data will give you a ballpark figure to compare your own website to. There will, of course, be a lot of different factors that impact your conversion rate—but this kind of reliable data will at least give you an indication of typical conversion rates, providing more context when you're evaluating the performance of your website.

An Analytics-first Approach to User Research

Hopefully this chapter has helped convince you that analytics has a big part to play in the user research process. I'm not proposing you *only* use analytics for research, as there's no substitute for talking to real users. But you can get a lot of really useful information from your analytics package, and this can give a solid foundation for your user research process.

As UXers, we know that understanding who our users are is absolutely key to creating a good experience. Analyzing your website's analytics data is a great way to improve that understanding.

Chapter **6**

Measuring and Reporting Outcomes

> The greatest value of a picture is when it forces us to notice what we
> never expected to see.
> — *John Tukey, American Mathematician*

So far, we've covered how to check that your analytics is set up correctly, how to use analytics data to identify potential problems, and how to use it for user research. These techniques, along with other UX methods, will help you to identify where you should make changes to your website, and what those changes might look like. Once you've made the changes to your site, don't stop there! You should look to measure the outcome of those changes and learn from the results.

Measuring the impact of your design changes is crucial. As IBM quality expert H. James Harrington said:

> Measurement is the first step that leads to control and eventually to improvement. If you can't measure something, you can't understand it. If you can't understand it, you can't control it. If you can't control it, you can't improve it.

Accurate measurement of UX can be difficult, but that doesn't mean you shouldn't try. This chapter will help you see the impact of your changes and prove the value of your work.

For ecommerce sites, you should be able to gain an understanding of how much additional revenue your changes have brought in. You may also want to measure other types of impact. For example, an ecommerce site may actually want to ensure there's no loss of revenue from a change rather than to gain additional revenue. You might also be more interested in increasing repeat custom, or improving non-financial goals.

For non-ecommerce sites, you'll want to accurately measure the number of additional goal conversions your designs are bringing in, so that you can report on the overall impact to the business.

Whatever the outcome of your changes, you need to be able to measure them so you can learn from them. This will help you make further improvements, or avoid making future changes that could negatively impact the UX of your website.

There are two ways to measure the impact of your changes using quantitative data: split testing, and before/after testing.

Split Testing

Once you've decided on the changes you'd like to make, the best way to test the impact of these is to use split testing. **Split testing** is a method of conducting controlled, randomized experiments with the goal of improving your site metrics. It's a way of comparing multiple versions of a web page (or web pages) to find out which one converts the best.

Split testing is the only way to really distinguish causation from correlation when evaluating the impact of your design changes.

There are three main types of split testing, described next.

A/B Testing

A/B testing is the simplest and most commonly used type of split testing. It's a method of website optimization in which the performance of a page—normally an original (or "control") page—and a variation (or variations) are compared to one another using your website visitors.

Users are "bucketed" into one version or the other to prove which variation performs the best. This is often measured by which leads to the highest number of conversions—though behavioral metrics, such as time on site and bounce rate, can be also be used to evaluate performance.

By tracking the way visitors interact with the page they're shown, and subsequent pages they visit, you can determine which version of the page is most effective.

The following diagram shows how a simple A/B test would work.

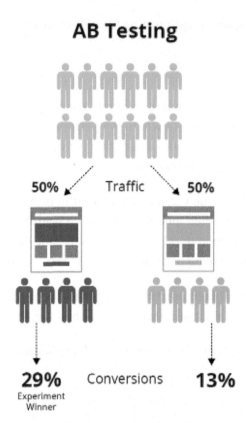

6-1. A/B test example (credit: Amy Cheng)

A/B tests often have more than one variation. These types of tests are sometimes referred to as **A/B/n tests** or **A/B/C/D tests**.

To demonstrate how an A/B test works, I'm going to use an ecommerce website that sells cameras as an example. The following screenshot is the original design:

6-2. Original design

In this example, we want to test whether changing the color of the "Add to basket" button changes user behavior. The following image shows how the variation design would look:

6-3. A/B test variation

This is a very simple test, and one which is unlikely to get good results! However, it demonstrates the principles behind A/B testing.

Many of the top split testing tools report that around 95% of split tests take the form of A/B tests, and as a result, people will often use the term "A/B test" to describe any type of split test.

Multivariate Testing

Multivariate testing uses the same comparison idea as A/B testing, but compares a higher number of variables, and reveals more information about how these variables interact with one another.

A multivariate test is run on a single page, but will evaluate changes to different elements. A multivariate test doesn't test a number of static designs against one another, but instead tests numerous versions of two or more page elements.

This may mean changing the text in a heading, changing a photo and changing the color of a button. For example, you might have three different headings, four different product photos and two different colors for the button. Combinations of these different elements are randomly shown to users until a winning variation is found.

As in an A/B test, traffic to a page is split between different versions of the design. The purpose of a multivariate test is to measure the effectiveness each design combination has on conversions or other performance metrics.

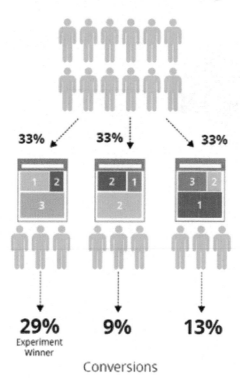

Multivariate Testing

6-4. Multivariate testing (credit: Amy Cheng)

Once a site has received enough traffic to run the test, the data from each variation is compared—not only to find the most successful design, but also to potentially reveal which elements have the greatest positive or negative impact on a users' interaction.

Going back to our camera website, the following screenshots show examples of how multivariate testing would work. Here we want to test with three different colored buttons, and three different product images, to find the best combination of the three.

6-5. Original design

6-6. An example variation

6-7. Another example variation

These are just two of the possible variations. In this example, because we're using three product images and three button colors, there would be a total of nine combinations, meaning nine different variations.

Multivariate testing is used much more rarely than A/B testing. It's best to approach split testing with a strong idea of what you're testing, and why. Your user research (and initial analytics analysis) will have given you a clear idea of where an improvement can be made, and what that improvement should be.

If not run correctly, multivariate testing can sometimes seem like a less targeted, almost random approach to split testing. Multivariate testing needs to be set up carefully, and should be based on clear reasoning, rather than just a desire to test as much as possible!

However, if you need to change multiple elements on a page, and have different variations you'd like to try out for each of them, multivariate testing could be the best choice. But keep in mind that, while multivariate testing reveals the interaction effect between multiple changing elements, it does require more traffic than A/B testing for the privilege.

Multi-page Testing

Multi-page testing is similar to A/B testing, except that, rather than making variations to a single page, the changes you make are implemented across several pages of a user journey.

As with A/B testing, site visitors of a multi-page test are bucketed into one version or another.

By tracking the way these visitors interact with the different pages (and their subsequent pages), you can determine which design variation is most effective.

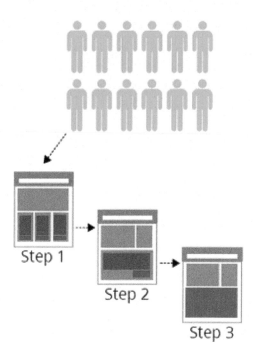

Multi-Page Experiment

Step 1

Step 2

Step 3

6-8. Multi-page test example (credit: Amy Cheng)

In the example of the camera website, we might simply keep the same colored buttons throughout the checkout process. This would be unlikely to have a big impact on the user experience, though.

Multi-page testing is less common than A/B testing, but will naturally appeal to us UXers. We like to consider the entire user experience, so focusing on several pages in the user journey will often make more sense than only changing elements on a single page.

Which Type of Split Test Should I Use?

The table below gives an overview of when to use each different type of split test.

Split test type	A/B testing	Multivariate	Multi-page
Use	Testing two or more variations of a web page	Testing different combinations of multiple elements on a web page	Testing changes to multiple pages on a user journey
Pros	<ul><li>The easiest type of testing to set up and manage</li><li>Offers statistically significant results faster than other forms of testing</li><li>Can be easily integrated with heatmapping tools</li></ul>	<ul><li>Allows for easy isolation of many small page elements and understanding their individual effects on performance</li><li>Measures interaction effects between independent elements to find compound effects</li><li>Follows a more conservative path of incremental improvement</li></ul>	<ul><li>Makes an impact across the user journey, and therefore has a bigger impact on the overall user experience</li><li>Avoids the inconsistent experience that other types of testing may lead to</li></ul>
Cons	<ul><li>May limit the amount of elements that can be tested</li><li>Hard to test the impact of changes in relation to each other</li></ul>	<ul><li>Major layout changes may not be possible</li><li>Can take a long time to reach statistical significance</li></ul>	<ul><li>Difficult to set up and plan due to their additional complexity</li><li>Hard to report on due to the need to analyze multiple pages</li></ul>

As you can see, each type of test has its own benefits, so think carefully about which one is best for your situation.

What to Consider When Setting up Split Testing

When you're ready to set up your split test, you need to pick a split testing tool. I touched on some of these in Chapter 1, but there are many other options available. I suggest you do your own research to find the right tool for your needs. The main areas to consider when choosing a tool are:

- cost
- features
- support
- ease of use
- reliability of results

 An Up-to-Date Overview

To get a good overview of the tools available, there's an excellent and regularly updated guide to split testing tools on Conversion Rate Experts[1].

Once you've chosen the right tool for your needs, you can set up your first split test. The following guidelines will help ensure your tests give you useful and accurate results.

Targeting Your Test

Firstly, consider who you want to be involved in your test. You can target visitors based on several different dimensions. For example, you may only want to include people from a specific country in your test, or you may want to target only returning visitors. Below are some of the common types of audience targeting you might include in your split testing tool:

- location (i.e. country or city)
- language
- new or returning

[1.] http://www.conversion-rate-experts.com/split-testing-software/

- device (e.g. mobile or desktop)
- browser type
- platform or OS
- traffic source (including referring URL)
- time of day

You may also be able to set up your own advanced targeting—perhaps based on users' cookie data.

As well as audience targeting, think about how many users you want to include in the test. If you have a website that receives a lot of traffic, you may want to limit the test to just a percentage of your audience, rather than including all users. You may also want to experiment with the percentage of users that are shown your variation(s). The following screenshot shows how the split testing tool Optimizely allows you to choose which percentage of your users are exposed to a test, and what percentage of them will be shown the control or variation(s).

Traffic Allocation

Specify the percentage of traffic that should be included in this experiment and be tracked for conversions. Visitors that are not included will not count towards your monthly quota.

50%
Included in experiment.

50%
Excluded from experiment.

Percentage of experiment visitors:

Original	50	%	Pause
Variation #1	50	%	Pause

6-9. Optimizely audience allocation

Choosing who is involved in your test can have a big impact on the results. For this reason, you should be careful about which users you choose to target.

Returning to our camera shop example, you may decide to target a test only at first-time visitors, as you don't want to risk changing the experience for the regularly returning users.

Choosing Your Goals

Split testing tools will require you to set up a goal, or goals, to use when reporting on the results of your tests. These follow the same principles as the goals you set up in your web analytics package.

For ecommerce websites (such as our camera shop example), it's likely that you'll want to set up goals that relate to purchases. You should set up goals that measure both the number of purchases and the order value. This will enable you to calculate the impact on the average order value and on the number of transactions. It's possible your changes may not lead to an increase in transactions, but may instead lead to an increase in the amount your users are spending when they make a purchase. In this case, you'll see an increase in the overall revenue being generated through the website.

For non-ecommerce sites, your goals will be similar to those you set up in your analytics (see Chapter 2). You may want to set up some additional test-specific goals too, depending on the change you're making.

Most split testing tools will allow you to set up multiple goals, though some limit how many you can set up. To keep analysis simple, I recommend only setting up the goals that are important to you. Some split testing tools can be integrated with your web analytics, meaning that you're able to see the impact of the test on a wide range of metrics without needing to set these all up in your split testing tool. I'll cover analytics integration in more detail later on in this chapter.

Duration of Test

Knowing how long to run a split test is crucial to getting accurate results. There are several factors to consider when working out how long a test should run. It can be a big mistake to "call" the results of a test too early. The purpose of running a split test is to accurately measure the performance of two or more different designs. You need to be sure the test is run in such a way that the results are a true reflection of each design's performance. You need to ensure the data reflects actual design choices, rather than factors outside your test, or even pure chance.

Before running a test, it's a good idea to work out roughly how long it will need to run. The first factor to consider is how the running time might impact your results. For example, if your test is only running on the weekend, this may favor a particular design. Also consider which part of the month your test will run. It's common for people to get paid at the end of each month, and this may impact their behavior on your website. For these reasons, it's often best, where possible, to run your tests for at least a month. This may not always be possible, or practical, but it's a good rule of thumb.

To decide on your test duration, also factor in how long it takes your users to convert. On some websites, users visit multiple times over a long period before converting. In this case, you'll need to work out the **purchase path length**—the number of days it takes your users to convert. The typical purchase path length can often be gleaned from your analytics package.

To do this in Google Analytics, navigate to **Conversions > Multi-Channel Funnels > Time Lag**. From here, you'll be able to see how long it takes your users to convert. The screenshot below shows 70% of people purchasing on the same day as their first visit.

Time Lag in Days	Conversions	Conversion Value	Percentage of total
			Conversions Conversion Value
0	9,625	$92,615.98	70.44% / 49.04%
1	384	$7,735.66	2.81% / 4.10%
2	196	$10,106.90	1.43% / 5.35%
3	151	$4,964.03	1.11% / 2.63%
4	177	$2,530.20	1.30% / 1.34%

6-10. Time lag report example

My recommendation here is to calculate how long it takes for at least 80% of your users to convert, and then ensure your test runs for at least this long.

In the case of our camera shop example, users are less likely to convert on their first visit than they would be for an ecommerce website selling cheap, everyday products. High-end cameras are likely to cost hundreds or even thousands of dollars, so users will be likely to return to the website over the course of several weeks before making a purchase.

Another important factor in knowing how long to run your test is the amount of traffic your website receives. If you're only getting 100 visitors a month, it will take a very long time to see a clear difference in the behavior of the users in your test. It may not be possible to run split tests on your site if you aren't getting enough visitors. The more visitors you can include in your test, the quicker you're likely to see a useful result. It's also important to remember that your test may only be running on a single page of your website. If your website receives a million visitors a month, but the page you're testing only receives a couple of hundred, this will mean split testing may not be possible here.

The minimal detectable effect will also impact on the sample size needed. For example, a test that has a 5% increase in conversion rate will need an exponentially higher sample size than one that has a 50% increase. While you can't predict uplift before you run a test, you can work out a minimum detectable effect based on what's going to give you a positive return. This allows you to work out a minimum sample size, which will help you estimate your minimum testing time. The A/B testing platform Optimizely has a useful calculator for working out sample sizes[2].

To produce a valid winner, your tests will need to reach statistical significance. I'll cover this in the next section on analyzing your results.

Analyzing Split Test Results

You've set up a test and are seeing good results coming in from it, but how do you know when it's time to declare that test a success? It's tempting to want to claim that a test has completed as early as possible, particularly if your suggested variation is winning! Ending a test enables you to go on to set up new tests, but

---

[2.] https://www.optimizely.com/resources/sample-size-calculator/

it's important that you wait until your test has a statistically significant winner before declaring it complete.

Agree Beforehand on What a Completed Test Means

People will often pounce on a small amount of data from a split test to back up their preferred outcome. Make sure you agree on what constitutes a "completed" test before you even set one up. The following information will help you decide the best way to do this, but it's important you get the agreements of all stakeholders involved in the test, to prevent them from calling the results too early.

There are several factors you need to consider when analyzing the results of your split testing.

Statistical Significance

Probably the most important factor to consider before calling the results of a test is whether it's reached statistical significance.

Statistical significance is reached when the difference is larger than can reasonably be explained as a chance occurrence. To use a simple example, if you suspect I have a pack of cards containing only spades, it won't prove anything if the first card I draw is a spade. If I replace the card, shuffle, and draw another spade, this could still be down to chance—although it's only a 6% chance with a normal deck of cards. If I draw ten spades in a row, chances are much higher this isn't a normal deck of cards (the odds of doing so being 1 in a million!).

Most split testing tools will calculate the likelihood of your results being down to chance. The tool will use all the data available on your site visitors and conversions to calculate how likely the changes you see in your conversions are down to your design changes alone.

Split testing tools will generally set a default statistical significance level for you. Your statistical significance level reflects how confident you need to be that results are down to your changes and not down to chance. For example, if you run a split test with a significance level of 95%, and you get a statistically significant result, you can be 95% confident that the results are real and not just caused by randomness. It does also means that there's a 5% possibility the changes are caused by chance alone. I recommend choosing a statistical significance level of 95% for your tests.

A good split testing tool will calculate statistical significance for you, but you'll also need to keep other factors in mind, such as those covered in the previous section. You'll also need to consider statistical power.

Reaching 95% statistical significance will protect against false positives—against finding a winner when there isn't one. However, statistical power is also needed to protect against false negatives—or not finding a winner when there is one—which is arguably just as important.

Some split testing tools will include statistical power calculations in their results reporting, in which case you don't need to worry about it. But some tools don't include it, and if the tool you're using just uses statistical significance, then to ensure accurate results, you'll need to use a separate sample size calculator to ensure you get enough participants and your test isn't "underpowered". Statistician and programmer Evan Miller has created a useful Sample Size Calculator[3] for this purpose.

Segmenting Your Results

When you're confident your test has reached a significant result, you can begin to analyze the data in more detail. Segment your results by different audiences to see how the test has performed for different types of users.

For example, you may see a 5% increase in conversions as a result of your test, and that's great. When you segment the results, however, you may discover there's been a 9% increase in conversions for desktop users, but a 2% drop in conversions for mobile users. This is a really important factor to be aware of, as it means your design has done even better than you thought for desktop users but needs rethinking on mobile.

[3.] http://www.evanmiller.org/ab-testing/sample-size.html

Ensure Your Sample Sizes Are Large Enough

As you segment the results of your split testing, make sure your sample size is still large enough for statistically significant results. Small segments may be less likely to reach statistical significance.

Integrating with Analytics

Some split testing tools will enable you to integrate your test data with your analytics package. This means you'll have access to the full range of metrics and will be able to analyze your results in much greater detail.

You'll be able to look at the impact on metrics like time on site, which can be very hard to set up as goals within split testing tools. You'll also be able to analyze user journeys in detail, to see how your design changes have impacted how users navigate through your site.

As well as integrating with web analytics packages, some tools will enable you to integrate with heatmapping tools.

This means you'll have a heatmap for the original design and one for each of your variations. This will enable you to see where your users are clicking, and how deep they're scrolling, for all of the designs in your test.

Before/after Testing

It may not be possible to set up a split test to monitor the impact of your changes. Some reasons for being unable to do so include:

- No budget for testing tools. (Some split testing tools can be expensive.)
- Not enough traffic to the web page to reach statistical significance.
- There are multiple or large-scale changes making a test setup difficult.
- The whole website has been rebuilt (though this doesn't always have to be a blocker!).
- Lack of any skills/experience in setting up tests. (This can obviously be overcome, but may be an issue if there's a looming deadline.)

In this situation, you may have to use "before/after" testing to measure the impact of your changes.

Before/after testing simply means comparing the data from before you made the design change to the data after you made the change. Ideally, you'll want to have your new design live for a reasonable amount of time. It's difficult to know how long this should be—but a month is generally a good rule of thumb, as this will cover a mixture of week days and weekends. Once your new design has been live for a month, you'll be able to compare a month of data for the new design against the previous month's data for the original design.

This approach is a lot less scientific than split testing, as there are multiple factors that could have caused the changes in behavior with the new design. But it is better than not measuring the impact of a new design at all.

Running Before/after Testing

To set up before/after testing, you can use the date comparison feature in Google Analytics—assuming the data you're measuring is being recorded there.

Make sure you're comparing like for like as best you can. This means including an equal number of weekends and weekdays in both the "before" and the "after" data. You should also be wary of public holidays or any other events that may have led to a spike or drop in your normal conversion rate. You may be able to shift your comparison dates slightly so that your data doesn't include these.

When comparing data over different time periods, you'll also need to consider seasonality. For a lot of ecommerce websites, for example, the revenue is likely to increase during the holiday season. Conversion rates may also change around that time. To get around this, you should analyze data from previous years (if it's available) to get an idea of how seasonality may be impacting your results. This is far from ideal, as there may have been changes to the website, industry or user behavior over the course of a year. As mentioned previously, though, it's better than running no analysis, and should at least give an indication of how your design changes have affected user behavior.

Problems with Before/after Testing

As I mentioned previously, before/after testing is far from ideal. There are lots of variables that can impact the results you're seeing, and if you're not careful, this kind of analysis can give inaccurate and misleading results.

If you communicate positive before/after test results to the whole business, and everyone starts using your positive change to inform their work on copy, design and so on, it could have a huge impact on the website as a whole. In this situation, you need to be very confident the increase you saw in your results wasn't caused by anything else that may have changed during that time.

The beauty of split testing is that it does an amazing job of limiting all other variables outside of the one you're trying to test. It's not perfect, but it's a lot better than before/after testing when it comes to giving clear, reliable results.

If you have to use before/after analysis, your aim should be to get as close to a split test as possible, by limiting or normalizing the variables. As well as ensuring you compare a large enough date range, you should also keep these things in mind:

- Organic search traffic is normally the most stable (apart from traffic from highly variable sources such as PPC and social media.)
- It's best to limit your analysis to users who've actually viewed your redesigned page.
- It's important to understand the wider company or market changes taking place, and use this information to normalize your data as best you can.

Analyzing Before/after Testing

As with most types of analysis, it's important to look beyond the obvious metrics. Conversion rate will be the starting point, but you should also analyze the impact on other aspects of user behavior, such as bounce and exit rates. Increases in bounce and exit rates may mean your users are less engaged, which could impact your long-term results. You need to be thinking about more than just the short period over which your changes have been live.

As with split testing, you should segment your results to see the impact on different user groups. This additional analysis can give you insight into exactly how the change you've made has altered the behavior of your users.

Before/after testing is far from the ideal way to analyze the impact of your design changes. But if you spend time carefully comparing the data, you'll often be able to get a sense of whether or not your change has been successful.

Design Changes and Returning Visitors

Whether you choose to report back the results of your changes using split testing or before/after testing, you'll want to consider how your returning visitors are likely to react to those changes.

Even if you're confident your new designs will give better results, there may be a downturn for a few days or a week as your existing users get used to the new designs.

A new design may not affect someone coming to your website for the very first time, but your returning users—particularly the most loyal ones—may be impacted, as people often struggle to cope with change. Those users may even follow something similar to the Kübler-Ross model of dealing with grief:

- **Denial**: people don't like change, and would prefer to stick with the old design.
- **Anger**: your users may be angry at you for changing a system they were comfortable with.
- **Bargaining**: users may try to make the new system work like the old one, or ask you at least to allow them access to the old system.
- **Depression**: remembering how much they liked the old design.
- **Acceptance**: realization that the changes have actually improved the website.

Every time major websites like Facebook or the BBC make big design changes, there's a lot of anger from their users. This phenomenon, sometimes known as "change aversion", occurs regularly. Whether it's changes to the Instagram logo, Twitter changing from a "star" to a "heart" for favorites, or a dramatic redesign of the iPhone UI when moving from one version of iOS to another, design changes can really get people worked up!

If the changes you're making are major, and you have a lot of loyal, returning users, you may need to run your tests for a longer period, to allow users to come to terms with the change. You may even want to consider targeting split tests only at new users, or at least segmenting your test results by new and returning users. Before you decide your design itself is the problem, just keep in mind that users may take time to adapt to change.

Reporting to Clients or Internal Teams

If your changes have shown interesting results, you'll want to share them with your clients and colleagues. There are various ways to report on the impact of your changes and share your results with others.

Reporting on the Results of Split Tests

Once you're confident your split test results are valid, you can report back to stakeholders. They may not be interested in statistical significance, but they'll be interested in the predicted impact to their business.

The impact to business should be measured not only in terms of increased conversion rate, but also by increased number of conversions over time, or saved revenue over time.

For ecommerce websites, stakeholders will naturally be interested in how much additional revenue your change has generated, as well as the likely ongoing increase in revenue it may lead to. Make sure to look beyond the test period, as the increased conversions the design change brings to your website won't stop when the test does (assuming you make the changes live on your site).

It's difficult to know how long your changes will continue to have a positive impact on conversions. I recommend calculating the predicted impact over the course of a year, but I wouldn't want to look any further ahead than this. I also recommend erring on the side of caution with your predictions. There's nothing worse that predicting high and falling short. Predicting low and exceeding expectations, on the other hand, is a great feeling!

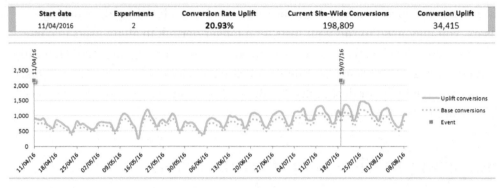

Start date	Experiments	Conversion Rate Uplift	Current Site-Wide Conversions	Conversion Uplift
11/04/2016	2	20.93%	198,809	34,415

6-11. Sample split test results report

Where possible, you should also consider retesting big changes, to ensure the results are still valid.

Reporting Before/after Results

Reporting on the results of before/after testing requires the use of the date comparison data in Google Analytics. You should compare significant metrics either side of making the changes and then present these.

You can make use of custom reports to pull out only the metrics that are important to you. Custom reports can be found in the top-level navigation of Google Analytics.

6-12. Custom reports in Google Analytics

Custom reports enable you to choose almost any combination of dimensions and metrics from Google Analytics to create a report that exactly matches your requirements. (The LunaMetrics blog gives a good overview of this, along with useful examples of custom reports[4].)

The following screenshot shows the setup for a custom report that looks at the data broken down by device types, including metrics on bounce rate, time on site and conversion rate.

6-13. Custom report setup in Google Analytics

Once you have the data, you need to consider how to present it. You could just share your custom reports, or you might want to export the data to Excel so that you can create graphs and run additional calculations. How you choose to present your results will largely depend on who you're presenting it to. Senior stakeholders may just want to see the impact on the bottom line, while members of the UX and Design teams may want to see more detail.

You should also share results outside the UX and Design teams. The learnings from your changes to onsite copy, functionality or designs could be useful to the Social Media, PPC or even Offline teams.

Ongoing Reporting

As well as reporting on the results of individual changes, you should also keep an eye on your data over time, to ensure your website is continuing to perform well. This section will cover some useful ways to keep up to date with your user behavior. You probably don't have the time to do "deep dive" analysis of your website analytics every day, so the following reports and techniques will help you efficiently maintain awareness of your website performance over time, without needing to spend all day looking at your data.

[4.] http://www.lunametrics.com/blog/2015/12/14/google-analytics-custom-reports/

Dashboards

One of the best ways to view the data that's important to you is to use the "dashboard" functionality in Google Analytics. **Dashboards** are a way of visually displaying the most important information needed to achieve your objectives. They provide a way of consolidating your data and reporting on it so key information can be monitored at a glance.

Dashboards in Google Analytics are made up of several different mini reports, known as **widgets**. Each widget takes one of the following forms:

- **Metric**: a single number, such as number of sessions
- **Timeline**: data over time, in the form of a line graph
- **Geomap**: data shown on a global map, using color to indicate areas of activity
- **Table**: one or two metrics based on a single dimension, shown in a table format
- **Pie**: data shown in a pie chart
- **Bar**: data shown in a bar chart

Dashboards can contain up to 12 different widgets, which means you can see a lot of data in one single page. Each widget can be created from scratch, so you only see the data that's relevant to your requirements.

Before you create your dashboard, it's a good idea to write down all the information you'd like to see on it, and how you want to break that down. You may want to focus heavily on ecommerce conversions, in which case you'll use metrics like conversion rate, number of transactions, average order values and total revenue. You can then think of how you want this data to be displayed, which may mean using metrics like country, device category and time of day.

Once your dashboard is created, you can get it sent to you by email at regular intervals. To do this, you need to click the Email button at the top of the dashboard and choose how often you want it emailed to you.

Don't forget, you can have several different dashboards. If you have a lot to report on, you may want to create different ones for different types of analysis. Examples of this include an ecommerce dashboard, an engagement dashboard and a technical dashboard.

Custom Reports

The custom reports we discussed earlier are similar to dashboards in some ways. They also enable you to manipulate your data to show you information based on your objectives. As mentioned earlier in this chapter, custom reports enable you to choose almost any combination of dimensions and metrics from Google Analytics to create bespoke reports. This means the reports you create can be as simple or complex as you need them to be.

Another advantage of custom reports is that you can use some metrics that aren't generally used in the standard reports. One area not currently represented in the standard reports is the time of day when users access your website. This dimension can be an important aspect of your users' behavior, but you'll need to create a custom report to make use of it.

Google Sheets

To gain even more flexibility in your data reporting, you may want to export your data. Data can be exported from within Google Analytics as `.csv` files, which can then be opened in Excel for further manipulation. Another option currently available is to import your data directly into Google Sheets. This functionality is available as an add-on to anyone with a Google account.

The add-on gives you a simple way to use the Google Analytics API without needing any coding skills. Using the add-on, you can:

- pull data from Google Analytics directly into a Google spreadsheet
- filter and segment your data
- compare data from different time periods
- schedule automated reports and dashboards
- create custom visualizations of your data using the chart functionality of Google Sheets

To find out how to set up Google Sheets analytics integration, read the official Google guide[5].

---

5. https://developers.google.com/analytics/solutions/google-analytics-spreadsheet-add-on

Google Data Studio

Launched in late 2016, Google Data Studio is a tool that allows you to turn your analytics data into informational, easy-to-understand reports using data visualization.

As mentioned in Chapter 1, Google Data Studio enables you to pull in data from multiple sources. As well as integrating with Google Analytics, Data Studio makes it easy to import data from platforms like YouTube and AdWords. You can also set up your own custom data sources.

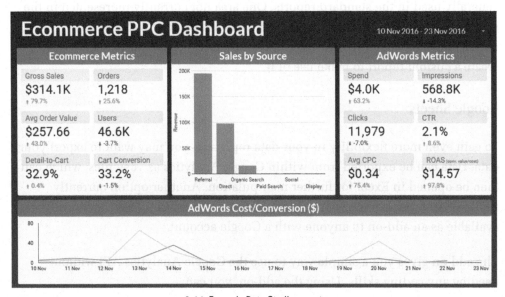

6-14. Example Data Studio report

While some effort is required to learn how to create reports with Google Data Studio, it's a great tool for generating reports truly customized to meet your needs.

Intelligence Events

So far, we've covered how to set up bespoke reporting. Google Analytics also attempts to identify important data trends automatically, using Intelligence Events. **Intelligence Events** reports monitor your website's data to detect significant statistical variations, and generate alerts when those variations occur. An example might be if your conversion rate was 50% less yesterday than the day before. This would generate an "event" that could be viewed in the Intelligence Events section of Google Analytics.

Intelligence Events reports can be found in the main, left-hand navigation of the Google Analytics interface. The Intelligence Events section is made up of "alerts" that relate to unexpected changes in your data. There are two different types of alert—automatic and custom. Automatic alerts are created by Google Analytics based on any unexpected changes to your data. These are listed in order of "importance", and an example of the automated reports table can be viewed in the following screenshot.

Automatic Alerts   Custom Alerts

	Metric	Segment	Period	Date	Change	Importance ↓
1.	Goal Conversion Rate	All Traffic	Weekly	Sep 11, 2016 - Sep 17, 2016	89%	
2.	Users	All Traffic	Daily	Sep 6, 2016	113%	
3.	Sessions	All Traffic	Daily	Sep 6, 2016	114%	
4.	Revenue	All Traffic	Weekly	Sep 11, 2016 - Sep 17, 2016	233%	
5.	Pageviews	Source: (direct)	Weekly	Sep 11, 2016 - Sep 17, 2016	219%	

6-15. Google Analytics Intellegence Events

As the screenshot shows, Google Analytics has noted that my conversion rate has risen by 89% week on week. It considers this to be the most important event that has occurred on my website during the last 30 days.

I don't often use the automatic alerts feature. While it can be useful for identifying big changes in your data patterns, the reports have no context, so won't be able to report accurately on the changes most important to you.

An alternative to using automated alerts is the Custom Alerts feature. As the name suggests, custom alerts enable you to create alerts based on the data that's most important to you. Custom alerts can be set up to email you when your data reaches a threshold you've specified. For example, you can set a custom alert to appear when traffic from the UK decreases by more than 25%. You can be alerted to changes in a wide range of metrics. Another example would be setting up an alert for when your daily revenue drops below a set figure.

Custom alerts mean you'll be alerted to significant changes in your data without having to log into Google Analytics. They give you a way of staying on top of your website performance with zero effort. Be careful, though, not to rely too heavily on these alerts. Continue to keep a close eye on your analytics to maintain a good understanding of how your users are behaving on your website.

Using Analytics for Continuous Improvement

However you measure and report on your data, you need to be thinking long term. If you have a successful result from your changes, don't just stop while you're ahead. Keep going, and aim for continuous improvement.

Sometimes you'll see big increases in performance as a result of your changes, while some changes will have a much smaller impact. Small increases add up, though, and you shouldn't overlook these "marginal gains".

The term **marginal gains** was popularized by Dave Brailsford, Performance Director for Team Sky and Team GB. His vision was to improve all aspects of his team's performance by just 1%, leading to an aggregation of marginal gains that would add up to something big. He was right. Bradley Wiggins won the Tour De France for Team Sky, and Brailsford's Olympic team won a staggering 70% of the cycling gold medals at London 2012 (before bringing home a similar haul in Rio 2016). Interestingly, "marginal gains" stems from the Japanese principle of Kaizen, which came about after the Second World War and is used by brands like Toyota to achieve ongoing excellence through continual change.

Whether your gains are significant or marginal, it's crucial that you're able to assess the impact they've had on the performance of your website.

Measuring and Reporting are Crucial

In this chapter, we've covered two ways to measure the impact of your design—split testing and before/after testing. It's vital that you're aware of the impact your changes have made so that you can learn from them.

As well as split testing, you should also use qualitative methods to further back up your results. Running user testing on new designs will add some qual to your quant—and, hopefully, give you confidence in your results.

Reporting the outcomes of your changes is a good way to show the value of your work, and also a good way to get others involved. Sharing a "big win" from your split test is a good way to show the impact design changes can have, and is likely to encourage others to offer input into future tests.

Conclusion

This concludes our look into using analytics to improve UX. There's a wealth of information available in your data to tell you *what* is happening with your website. You can use your analytics data to find issues with your website and to improve your user research. You can then use analytics techniques to evaluate and measure the success of your designs.

Thanks for reading this book. I hope it's inspired you to take an analytics-first approach to your UX process. Remember, quantitative analysis shouldn't replace qualitative research methods. Instead, the two should work in tandem to give you the best possible results for your UX methods.

Next Steps

We've covered a lot in this book, but don't be overwhelmed! I'll end with some ideas to get you started with integrating analytics data into your UX process.

1. Sign up for a Google Analytics account if you don't have one already. You can get an account for free, and getting set up is as easy as adding a line of code to your pages.
2. Once you've got your account, you'll need to check that it's working as expected. Use tools like GAchecker.com to ensure the code is running correctly on all pages of your site.
3. Set up custom configuration for your analytics. Look into setting up goals, events, internal search, content grouping and demographics reports. Also add filters to remove visits from spam/bot sources and your own IP address.

4. Once you've customized your account, familiarize yourself with the interface and get comfortable with the key reports.

5. To begin identifying where you should focus your UX efforts, identify underperforming areas using a range of reports. Remember to segment your data to see if any of your different user groups are experiencing issues. At this stage, also consider using data from heatmapping tools to give you even more insight.

6. Next, use your analytics data to help with your user research process. Your analytics package will tell you where your users are coming from, the languages they speak, and their demographics (such as age and gender). You'll also be able to analyze the behavior of your different user groups, in order to further inform your research.

7. You can use this research to help you to create personas, and you can recreate these personas in your analytics package to see how they're behaving on your site.

8. If you make changes to your website, use your analytics data to monitor how they've impacted user behavior, particularly in relation to conversions. You may want to use split testing tools to help measure this too.

9. Finally, consider how you're going to report back the results of the changes you've made. Using custom reports and dashboards can help you here.

Appendix A: Google Analytics Glossary

Annotation	a comment on a graph about an incident that may have had a big impact on your data.
Benchmarking reports	a way to compare your stats to those of your peers.
Bounce	a session with only one page view.
Cohort	set of users sharing a characteristic and time frame.
Content Group	a data set segregated by URL, screen name, page title etc.
Conversion	when a user completes a goal.
Custom Report	a report based on dimensions and metrics that you specifically choose.
Dashboard	a custom page showing a number of widgets.
Demographics	in Google Analytics, demographics reports contain data on the age and gender of your users.
Dimension	the name of a metric, normally the first column in a report table.
Entrance	the first page view of a session.
Event	something that happens on a website but triggers no HTTP request (such as a view of an embedded video).
Exit	when someone leaves your site.
Exit Rate or Exit %	percentage of exits from a specific page or pages.
Filter	exclude data (such as requests from your IP address) at the point of collection.
Funnel	a visualization of a path taken by visitors as they complete goals or conversions.
Goal	a form of conversion, fired and recorded in Google Analytics when a user completes a predefined behavior.
Landing Page	the page on which a visitor enters your site.
Metric	data collected by Google Analytics; the numbers that appear in reports next to Dimensions.
New visitor	a user that has visited your site once during a specified time period.
Page Value	the monetary value of a page as calculated by Google Analytics (for example, Transaction Revenue ÷ Unique page views in ecommerce).

Pages per session	the mean number of webpages viewed during your sessions.
Pageview	when an HTML page is accessed.
Remarketing	showing people adverts for the site they've recently exited.
Returning visitor	a visitor who has made at least one visit to at least one page on your site previously in the set time period.
Segment	data from a group of users who share some attributes.
Session	the period during which someone actively engages with your site, aka a "visit".
Site Search	internal site search, a feature allowing users to submit a search query.
Unique Pageviews	the number of sessions that included a visit to a page.
Unique Visitor	someone who goes to your site, aka a "user".
Visit	a previously used term for a Session.
Visitors flow	the visitors flow report shows how users have navigated through your site.
Weighted sort	a way of prioritizing data by importance instead of numerical order.
Widgets	small snapshots of data (shown as tables, graphs etc.) that make up a dashboard.

Lightning Source UK Ltd.
Milton Keynes UK
UKOW07f2113130117
292054UK00001B/1/P

9 780994 347077